Dear friend

A 90-DAY DEVOTIONAL

To all the best friends in the world...

• • •

those ones who make you laugh out loud, love harder,
do things you never knew you could,
dream without limits and always find time for coffee.

INTRODUCTION

Hi, friend!

Today is a new day— a gift that you will never open again.

Today could be one of those "once in a lifetime" kind of days or one of those where you are just really thankful the sun came up and set and you didn't have to worry about it. Each day people wake up and life seems to happen all around them. Life has its pace for each person, through those "just so happens" and through all the ups and downs. Some days are full and rich while on others we hit our pillow wondering what was the point. Whichever day is, it falls in the midst of 365 you were gifted this year.

One thing I found in common from conversations with friends is that we are looking for a good friend to walk with, talk to or to share an adventure with. You know, the one friend that sticks through the good and the bad. One who doesn't always offer an answer but sits with a sympathetic ear. A friend who won't let us settle for just anything, but truly believes and hopes for good things to come our way.

As I write this to you, I hope it comes into your hands when you need a good friend and you find me in the pages. And for those days when you say— "This is someone else's letter. She wrote this for my friend." I hope you will in turn be a good friend to that someone in your circle by sharing. If that means ripping out a page, then rip away! You, friend, **get to live it or give it.**

I believe these letters will encourage your relationship with God and people. I am praying for you as you read these pages, asking God to do all the little things that make the biggest impact in your heart. I pray God will strengthen, encourage, and add to your life in small and big ways as you read and listen for His voice through my words.

In the book of Mark, Jesus told the people, 'If you can! All things are possible for one who believes." May you take one page at a time, and fully believe God to do the impossible. Believe today, whichever day on the calendar it is, that God will Author this day and your story in such a way that it is fresh, full of life and will only get better!

Life with God is so so good!

Love
Becca

It just so happens on a Sunday morning I was traveling home and I stopped for coffee. In the Starbucks line, I eavesdropped on a conversation two people were having on why they were in a Starbucks line on that Sunday morning instead of at church. They were so glad there was a Thursday night service they could attend so they could have their weekends... it was so convenient. My heart was so saddened. When did God become a convenience?

Are we a part of a generation that wants God based on our own convenience?

How much is My relationship with God based on convenience?

How often does that relationship cost me anything at all?

Do I find myself in church only when the timing is my schedule?

Do I serve only when I have nothing else to do?

Do I read your Bible only when I need a quick pick me up or when I want to post something on instagram?

Then Jesus told his disciples, "If anyone would come after me, let him deny himself and take up his cross and follow me." Matthew 16:24

Faith isn't convenient. Love isn't convenient.

Picking up that cross of mine isn't anything close to convenient.

Did you get that? I have to pick up my cross. The very symbol of death. My cross... it's not just thrown on my back. It's not just given to me. It sits there each and every day, waiting to see what I will do.

Am I truly willing to pick it up, putting fully to death my agenda and live out His?

I find myself at a crossroads multiple times a day— my way or His way. Some days I am sooooooo willing; some days I am soooooo not willing.

Which one will I—or you—decide for today: Willing or unwilling? (Circle one)

Life is full of places we were created to step into that will take lots of grit, love, endurance, patience. Those places are not convenient. Nothing is convenient in our relationship with God. NOTHING.

When was the last time you did something as a disciple of Christ that wasn't convenient?

• • •

So, what do you choose? Does God have full access, to not only your heart to save you, but to your hands, your feet, your calendar, your "TO DO" list, your mornings, middays, nights, weekends, your mouth, your money, your family, your ears...

Taking up my cross moment by moment, day after day, thinking of you,

Love

Rebecca

NOTES

_____

_____

_____

_____

_____

_____

_____

_____

_____

_____

_____

_____

_____

_____

_____

_____

Dear friend

DAY TWO

__ / __ / __

Don't let what has been common to man become your normal. God's kingdom is so much greater than the common! Resist the temptation to stay in the common.

Take hold of who God is today! Every day Jesus was walking on the earth, there was a draw on His faith. As He went in and out of towns, sat beside watering holes, walked in the streets, attended weddings, ate a meal, went to the temple...each place and each activity provided a specific moment for his faith to break onto the surface. The love God put in him couldn't be contained in His flesh; there were moments each day, for release.

> For I have not spoken on My own authority; but the Father who sent Me gave Me a command, what I should say and what I should speak. And I know that His command is everlasting life. Therefore, whatever I speak, just as the Father has told Me, so I speak." John 12: 49-50

We are called to walk the same earth that Jesus did, doing things like going shopping, eating at a Chick-fil-A (or your fav), attending a wedding celebration, a workshop, a funeral; eating in a lunchroom, running a marathon,... we walk down many paths in our lives. The question is— is your faith ready to be released wherever you go, whatever you do?

Each day lived for Christ should carry at least an opportunity to live out our love and our faith. Not only believing for crazy big stuff— a car, healing, a house, children— but watching for all the opportunities. We need to see God step into our everyday life, like when Jesus rested at the town well and met the Samaritan woman... and changed her life (Check out John 4:6-26). The relationship you have with God is for each morning you wake up, each time you walk down the stairs, each day you live every minute (1440, to be exact).

Do you live like a person of faith? **Do you ever allow your faith to show itself?** If someone watched you for 24 hours, would they know that you allowed God to use you at any time?

I am speaking to myself, too. Sometimes days can pass and I don't even pay attention to what God is asking me in my immediate circumstances because I'm looking too far ahead to what's coming or just surviving the moments. IS that the life of Christ.

Christ lived out His call, every moment. Even when the disciples were trying to rush him into the future, He wouldn't have it. (Read the story of Lazarus in John 11:1-44). Jesus told his disciples this circumstance was about God being glorified, not rushing ahead of God's perfect timing. He didn't fear what the situation looked like, or His faith not working, because He chose to be close to the one who wrote each day and let His father work through him.

Jesus said, "Did I not tell you that if you believed you would see the glory of God?' So they took away the stone. And Jesus lifted up his eyes and said, 'Father, I thank you that you have heard me. I knew that you always hear me, but I said this on account of the people standing around, that they may believe that you sent me." John 11:40-42

Your days are written (Psalm 139:16). God is in the pages, the timelines, the Instagram stories. He is walking with you, but won't step over the boundaries of faith you have set. You have to present your faith to God, be available, and let God do what He does. Jesus' example was our example... every day. Each place and in any moment, our faith has a mandate. Let's allow our faith to display the glory of God and make Him known so that someone might come to Jesus.

When God is calling you into an uncommon place, live supernaturally!

Love
Bec

NOTES

_____

_____

_____

_____

_____

_____

_____

_____

_____

_____

_____

For you died, and your life is hidden with Christ in God. Colossians 3:3

Today I'd like to talk to you about coming into Jesus, abiding by Him. Imagine God speaking these words directly to you:

> "Beloved, when you are willing to step outside of yourself and step into Me, you will find a new place of anointing. You will be able to live out what I have purposed for you. Your boss might have specific things for you to do, so prepare yourself to accomplish the task. Mine is the same type of assignment. One that requires you to be completely surrendered to living, breathing and walking out the unfolding My unfolding plans without knowing everything, for you would end up stopping in your tracks. You CAN come to a place of leaning into me and trusting that I am working in each and every situation. I am calling you to live and move in ME, not in your own flesh. It is common for mankind to live in the flesh and do what the flesh wills. But I am the Living God and my Will is for My Holy Spirit to take over your flesh, to fill you, surround you and guide you through your day."

> ~Your Heavenly Father

Do you feel empowered?

I strongly encourage you to not live in competition with His Spirit. Your flesh will arise and say you have no need for the Spirit of the Living God. But competing with God's will can only lead to failure. Your flesh has limits; it is only equipped and fashioned to do so much. In fact, our flesh always leads to death.

Your first breath just so happens to be your first breath towards death. It just so happens to be. Yet God never wanted death or separation from you— the flesh and sin created that space.

God wants a moment when you take off that old, dying flesh and exchange it for the mystery of salvation— receiving a body that is incorruptible.

But now you must put them all away: anger, wrath, malice, slander, and obscene talk from your mouth. Do not lie to one another, seeing that you have put off the old self with its practices. Colossians 3:8-9

Can you identify time when your flesh is leading you day after day? It's pretty much constant— you can't get away from your own flesh. Yet **God wants all of you**....each inch and every moment. What is holding you back from giving Him full control over your life? Is God always going to be your last resort? Why not step into Christ living through you and let Him overwhelm you with the life He has designed?

Living in His life.

Becca Pove

NOTES

_____

_____

_____

_____

_____

_____

_____

_____

_____

_____

_____

_____

_____

_____

_____

_____

_____

_____

dear friend

There are days when we head into our day with specific expectations.

Maybe even today you anticipate it will unfold a certain way— Today I will have happy children, I will laugh more than I ever have. I will make amazing food. My house will stay clean. I will get a tan. I will burn more calories. I will write more…

I have found that most days aren't exactly as I planned, or expected, because God was involved. Some days, I think, "This wasn't supposed to happen," but then I remember He was helping shape my day. He was there doing things behind the scenes and leading me. Most of the time, I love curveballs because they turn a normal day into an exciting, unexpected adventure!

> *For it is God who works in you both to will and to do for His good pleasure.*
> *Philippians 2:13*

The other day I was planning an ordinary play date with one of my friends and her children and God opened up so much more. I headed out with preset plans and ideas but God said, "I have something better." On the way home, I thought, "That wasn't what I had planned at all. I am so glad that God had a different plan!"

> *For we are His workmanship, created in Christ Jesus for good works, which God*
> *prepared beforehand that we should walk in them. Ephesians 2:10*

What do you do with the unannounced adventures in your day? Do you stay in peace when things get turned around? Do you find yourself trusting that God will work it out, or do you get all crazy and throw up your hands?

God is the peace you need today.

He creates spaces and things to happen beyond our understanding, but it is for good. He wants to be the peace we need in every moment.

> *Oh Lord, you will keep in perfect peace all who trust in you,*
> *all whose thoughts are fixed on you. Isaiah 26:3*

When you feel a lack of peace today, know God is there and His peace is available. His peace will create excitement if you let it. It will make you wonder what God is up to. Get excited if plans change; it just means He has better plans in store! As a planner, I love planning unexpected surprises for the ones I love.

I know God is the same way with me… and you.

Trusting the God of curveballs,

Are you desperate today? Remember 2020? Empty shelves, no toilet paper… We found ourselves being overwhelmed with lack and in distress, but nothing compared to what you read in 2 Kings 6:24-33. Samaria was being besieged by an enemy, so no food could be brought into the city. They were willing to boil their children for food. Donkeys' heads were being sold for 10 months of earnings. Even doves' dung was being sold for food. Imagine the fears, the exploiting, the death, the fight for life. How long could what was happening keep happening?

The Word of the Lord came to Elisha in the middle of the great distress in the land. Between the cries, the Word of the Lord came…It spoke to the circumstances and declared utter, crazy change. Something that wasn't possible within their understanding.

Then Elisha spoke: 'Hear the Word of the Lord: Thus says the Lord, Tomorrow at this time a seah (six quarts) of fine flour will be sold for a shekel (½ ounce of silver) and two seahs of barley for a shekel at the gate of Samaria." 2 Kings 7:1-2

Elisha, God's prophet, had a message of hope that tomorrow they would move from famine to more than enough. Could it be? Was the picture drawn before them possible? Would they believe the Word of God's prophet, or were the walls holding of fear and lack blinding their vision?

This is the best part…the provision was actually right outside the same gates that were now imprisoning them. Just outside those gates were the enemy's resources. It was actually there all along, they just didn't/couldn't see it until some desperate men ventured out of the gates and discovered God had scared away their enemy who left behind all their provisions!

That's just like God, He is always there. For real. Your Bible is full of every promise that has already been purchased for you. It's been there before you even found yourself in need. It's yours. I love that about God! Sometimes in the darkest moments, we get the ability to actually see Jesus for who He is, to see God's provision surrounding you. He hasn't left you nor forsaken you.

He is your Answer.

For your Father knows the things you have need of before you ask Him. Matthew 6:8

When you find yourself in desperate places, desperately want what God has for you in that very moment. I'm praying for you, friend!

Trusting God when there seems to be no way,

Love
Rebecca

I was reading Luke 1:5-24 this morning. Check it out!

Zechariah prayed for his wife to have a baby. How long did he pray? We actually don't know. Luke 1:6 says:

They both were righteous before God, walking blamelessly in
all the commandments and statutes of the Lord.

They were good people; loving God and living for him, still life was not perfect, not simple. Not having a baby was considered to be God's displeasure or judgment. Think about a year of praying and waiting… the discouragements, the disappointments. Yet Zechariah faithfully served the Lord as a temple priest.

God met Zechariah in the Temple where he was burning incense.

God strategically placed him in a position to be inside the temple to hear from the Lord. God wanted the message to come into the space man created to reach beyond what was. Luke 1:13 says:

But the angel said to him, "Do not be afraid, Zechariah, for your prayer has been heard,
and your wife Elizabeth will bear you a son, and you shall call his name John."

Zechariah was in the presence of an angel. I love that the angel says, "for your prayers have been heard." He must have not quit praying, but childlessness held enough disappointment so that he responded in unbelief to the angel who told him his wife would conceive and bear a son. The plans of God were beyond what the natural could do. Only God could make a baby when nature said it's not possible.

Zecharaiah let the angel know all the ways it couldn't happen (Luke 1:18). Gabriel, the angel, responded by saying he (Gabriel) had just been the presence of God. (Luke 1:20). Zechariah was silenced by God for a time because of his unbelief.

Yet God continued to work through Zechariah. John was conceived, which took faith and passion from both him and Elizabeth. God's desire to answer and honor their faithfulness. Life changed. The richness of what God did for them was incredible! Bringing the prophecy of Isaiah 40:3 into fulfillment, God revealed the plan He had for their son, John the Baptist: "The voice of one crying in the wilderness: "Prepare the way of Lord; make straight in the desert a highway for our God."

The silence that Zechariah walked through should speak to our unbelief. Let your faith be lived out loud. Whatever God speaks over you, let your response be, "Yes." Keep strengthening your faith by reading the Word. Let the Word be consistently in your grasp. Don't let unanswered prayers keep your faith chained in a position that pulls it to unbelief. Guard your heart from unbelief. **Choose to believe God at His Word.** God is fulfilling His Word through His people. We get to be part of that! Stir your faith and belief. God is still answering prayers and fulfilling His Word. Pause and pray—believe

BIG! He will answer, my friend.

Don't give up,

NOTES

How are your friendships?

Have you ever defined friendship? Friendship will consist of personal space for freedom of time and feelings. Friendship takes time and effort with both sides actively working. Friendship should consist of prayer— both for and with friends.

What makes a person a friend?

Do you have friends who know you deeper than what you post on Facebook?

Do your friends push you and challenge you in your walk with God?

I recently heard a song with this thoughty line: "You can't make old friends." It's true. Acquaintances definitely come and go, but friends stay around. Do you have friends who really know you? Can you name your top 5?

Friendships we long for always have a starting point but gradually grow into old friends. **Friendship is valuable and involves the heart.** Through friendship, trust is nurtured and tested; not something to take lightly or passively. Are you real in your friendships? God created and spoke about friends for you and me.

What kind of friend are you? Pause and ask God to make you a better friend. Our friendship with God should only add to the friendship we have with others.

Jesus had friendship that filled the above criteria. He didn't attach to just anyone. He was specific. He chose and walked with the same 12 guys for 3 ½ years of his ministry on earth. He called them, loved them, listened to them, challenged them, provoked them, encouraged them, pushed them, fed them (spiritually and physically), and enabled them to see differently. Do you wish and pray for friends like that? Are there friendships that you need to cut out, and others you need to take the next step deeper? Proverbs 17:17 says, "A friend loves at all times." Are you that kind of friend?

Greater love has no one than this, that someone lay down his life for his friends. John 15:13

Jesus expressed the greatest love on the earth when He lay down His life for you and me. Jesus wants a real friendship with you, where He shares His heart and you share yours. Out of His longing for friendship with you and me, He died in our place. He lay down his life, and we lay down our lives. He doesn't need something from you, and you don't have to be perfect and tidy. You can come in your mess— in your sweatpants— He finds everything about you beautiful. The longer you are friends with someone, the less you see the outside appearance....you see and share the depth of their hearts. When He first saw you, He saw what friendship with you could look like. He saw the joy you could bring Him. He saw the adventures you could share. He saw what you could create with Him as your greatest support and cheer leader. He saw the places along the way that you would need to be loved and carried through. He saw the hurt you would experience and wove mercy into who He was for just those moments. He saw the needs you would have, and He came with more than enough to see you through. He made things along the way that would cause you to wonder and be awestruck by. He wrote letters about His love for you to read. He made ways for nothing to stand between you and Him. John 21 gives us a look at the friendship Jesus had with Peter. He wants friendship with you. Check out these questions to stir your heart for the more in your friendships:

1. Who do you process with?

2. Who speaks into your now and future?

3. Who do you bounce your God ideas off of?

4. Who has the "sit down and shut up" card in your life?

5. Who do you trust with YOU? The most vulnerable/raw parts of you?

6. Who can tell you "that wasn't God"?

7. Who accepts you where you are, but refuses to allow you to stay there?

8. Who can identify your blind spots?

9. Who calls out what's on the inside of you when you don't see it yourself?

10. Who celebrates you?

@reshena_is_loved

Friendship is a gift! I am thankful we share that gift,

NOTES

_____

_____

_____

_____

_____

_____

_____

Dear friend

I've been thinking about the story of Jesus walking on the water. Most people know it to a degree, but perhaps there's more to it. Would you set aside any thoughts you have about it, clearing your mind for a fresh perspective. No matter how many times you have or if you've never read the story, please take time right now to read Matthew 14:22-33.

The picture is that a terrible storm is happening all around them. Jesus' disciples were afraid. That picture can be symbolic of so many things happening in our lives. If there isn't currently a storm happening in your life, I pray this will give you confidence when a storm does hit.

Jesus sent his disciples ahead, knowing they would end up in the middle of a storm. God is not unaware of your storms. Some storms create places to work out our faith, perseverance and guts.

As Jesus was coming close to the guys in the boat, they thought that He was a ghost. In the middle of a storm, sometimes Jesus doesn't appear the way you want Him to. You want Him to be the calm, and He wants to be the Peace within you, causing you to step out in the middle of the miracle.

Their idea of who He is wasn't clear. Jesus told them to go to the other side of the lake, but all they saw was the waves, winds, and rain. Sometimes our problems seem so vivid that God gets blurred. Truth is, even if they couldn't see him, He was there. In the midst of their distress, they had to listen. He spoke to them, "Take Heart, it is I...do not be afraid." Basically, today we can't rely on what we can see, but on knowing the voice of the One who can break through anything that is happening. We have to be willing to let Jesus' voice settle anything that comes against what God has spoken to us.

As the story continues, Peter said, "If it is you then command me to come out onto the water."

Peter still couldn't clearly see Jesus, so He had to trust His voice. Let your vision of Him get clearer the closer you get.

We can create boundaries for what we want God to do that don't require us to step out of the boat. God is calling us out of our boat. The command is still the same: COME. Don't hesitate! Don't delay! Don't let your natural vision drive you into doubt and fear. Don't let storms stop you from seeing all God can do. It just so happens Jesus didn't stop the storm when Peter hopped out of the boat. When fear and doubt started weakening Peter's faith out on the water, Jesus simply grabbed Peter's hand to steady him, and they kept walking together, in the midst of the raging storm.

The wind ceased once they got back into the boat. God wanted Peter's faith to grow, not die in the middle of the miracle.

So what's keeping you in the boat, my friend? When are you going to step out of the safe spaces you have created that only limit a limitless God? The disciples were skilled fishermen and the boat was crafted by a man, both in their comfort zone of the comfortable. Get out of the boat when He says," COME."

His desire is for your life to be full of unnatural, crazy faith!

In the storm, stop staring at the wind and waves, stop blaming God for not showing up how you wanted Him to. Start listening to Him and step out with the same attitude of Peter: "Jesus I just want to be where you are, storm or not."

The Lord wants to do some crazy awesome things in our lives, but we must be willing to take the first step!

Hopping out of the boat, *Love Bec*

NOTES

_____

_____

_____

_____

_____

_____

_____

_____

_____

_____

_____

_____

I woke up this morning feeling so impressed to challenge you. Are you living out what God has put in you? Are you using your faith daily or living in fear of your faith being exposed? Faith is unseen, yet should be evident every day. I encourage you to live your faith out loud!! Do you watch others live their faith and think, "I will cheer them on?" Is cheering someone in their faith why God gave you faith? Do you want more...more of the living God? Are you taking steps towards Him no matter what the cost? The unknown 'more' can be one of the biggest risks, with the greatest rewards.

Again, I am reminded of Peter. First, Peter didn't have it all together. Hopefully that encourages you, but to his credit, he wasn't intimidated when his reason wasn't enough. Let's revisit our passage from yesterday: Matthew 14:22-33.

There were 12 dudes on the boat. The storm was wicked. They were fearful and when they looked out into the darkness, they thought they saw a ghost. There are times when we look out and all we see is darkness and fear staring us in the face. The circumstances of life and hardships can be overwhelming and make us feel like, at any moment, we could drown. The disciples (Jesus' closest followers), were freaking out in the boat. Except for Peter...he looked past the storm and saw something different. He saw Jesus, his friend. He didn't let the wind and waves stop him. He didn't have to figure it all out. He just looked to the One that was in that space and could change all the things that shouldn't be able to be changed. He let Jesus decide what could or could not happen. Jesus called him into the storm so he went willingly. He left behind 11 other guys that could have stepped into the same moment, but fear and doubt stopped them. Peter pushed beyond what anyone else had ever done by obeying just one word: Come! So... will you be one of 11 who stay on the boat or will you step out with Peter?

Peter wasn't without fear...he just exercised obedience, despite his fear. Jesus didn't just draw Peter out to the dark sea, He took Him through the raging seas, brought him to Himself, walked him back to the boat and silenced the storm. It's time to stop focusing on the storm! We have too many believers sitting in a boat in the middle of the storm, and panicking without seeing the unseen God, Who is ready to take us into the deep with Him. When you let your faith jump, you will find that God can change the very elements and cause you to walk into impossible places.

Trust that when God calls you into a place of the unknown, He will be there every step of the way, drawing you closer to Himself.

Following the voice of God doesn't mean that storms won't exist, it means to keep taking steps and watch God do a mighty work in and through you. What is your faith reaching towards? Where is your trust...in the boat or the power of God? Is it with what your friends are willing to do? Is your faith confined to what seems like a safe place? (Think about it, the 11 disciples who stayed frozen in fear were not safe in the boat either) I want to be wherever Jesus is!

Jumping out of the boat, even if I am afraid,

Love
Rebecca

NOTES

dear friend

Part of my journey included hitting a crossroads with my husband.

We were living in Oklahoma, and God was kicking us out (literally, I'm not joking). Everything in our life started going crazy; everything normal and comfortable was stripped away. We heard Him tell us to go, yet kept holding on… that's where we were. We had two options: move here or there. Romaro said we were going to move here and I said there. What do you do when your spouse wants to go where you believe you shouldn't? We battled day and night. We couldn't find a compromise. We couldn't find peace. I kept seeking counsel from this one and that one… most people said "Just stay." We didn't have that option. One of my girlfriends gave me wisdom that I chose to treasure and embrace. She said: God made the dynamics of marriage, and if I, as wife, submitted to Romaro (even if I felt it was wrong), God would cover me. Romaro would have to stand in front of God, in front of me. He was the ultimate authority in our marriage. At that moment I chose to trust God in my life and trust that He would lead us through Romaro. This surrender wasn't a miracle moment. It was a journey I walked out. Imagine how difficult it was driving in the car, following a moving truck to a location I didn't think was right. Everything in me wanted to turn around. Everything in me was screaming! I almost felt like I was going to crumble and spiral into a mess.

Maybe you have felt like this in a similar situation or another when it's hard to submit, hard to trust, hard to be ok. I heard a podcast say, "You can stay and spiral into your mess or you can choose to live and thrive." Another crossroads. I had to make a choice: would I crumble and be useless or thrive and grow? I made a choice that day, followed by the next day, and the rest of that week…month…year. I trusted that God was on my side and working on my behalf, because I chose His way in my marriage.

Why was it so important to learn to submit to my husband, when a few years later he would be gone? Why?! I asked God, "Why?!? What did you really want from me?" I felt God said, "If you are willing to submit to your husband, I know you will be willing to submit to Me." God was working on me through all of this. He was so kind in leading me closer to Himself through these crossroads. Perhaps you are facing some hard decisions right now. I encourage you to trust God with your/His plans.

Never give up believing that He is working.

If we do it His way, He will show up.

When you find yourself at a crossroads, look for Jesus and follow His lead. He can make things beautiful in the middle of your uncertainty. God blessed us tremendously in our new home. I made amazing friends and connected with a local church. I grew in my relationship with God. Really, I "felt" so so so in love with God!

And guess what? God moved us again 15 months later to the state I had originally thought was the right one. Romaro apologized to me, confessing that he knew where we were supposed to be here all along, but at the time he just couldn't do it. I was deeply touched by his humility and that God made things right.

Viewing crossroads as opportunities,

NOTES

_____

_____

_____

_____

_____

_____

_____

_____

_____

_____

_____

_____

_____

_____

_____

_____

_____

_____

_____

_____

There are times when we really do not know what to say to people. Do you give advice without considering what the Lord is saying? There are times when our own advice could lead someone down the wrong path. I advise you to just not say anything until you consult the Holy Spirit.

The right word at the right time is like a custom-made piece of jewelry, And a wise friend's timely reprimand is like a gold ring slipped on your finger. Reliable friends who do what they say are like cool drinks in sweltering heat—refreshing! Proverbs 25:11-13

More than your compassionate words, friends need your willingness to listen to the Lord, wait to hear from Him and then bring them His counsel. The amazing truth is that God already knows the whole story. He authored it. He has the details to a T. Ask Him, "How do I help? What words do you want me to give to help?"

The Lord God has given me the tongue of those who are taught, that I may know how to sustain with a word him who is weary. Morning by morning he awakens; he awakens my ear to hear as those who are taught. As you awaken, you need to know what God is wanting your tongue to say and not to say. We have to have to have the right words that will bring the sustaining power. Isaiah 50:4

Before you speak, ask what God wants you to say and not to say.

Then you will have the right words to bring the sustaining power.

I am so struck with the idea that God is our Wonderful Counselor! He is going to counsel us in each and every area. Not just in the majors but in the minors, too. We must be willing to seek the counsel of the Lord; then, awakened to what God is speaking, we can impart His Word to someone in need.

Do you begin your day with the thought that God could give you a verse or encouragement for someone else? We may not know whose path we will cross, but God knows. Let God awaken His Spirit in you to put words in your mouth to speak for those you will cross paths with. Learning to listen has to be consistent, each and every day. Strive to be more attentive to God's voice in every moment, not just when you draw aside to listen. Pray each morning, "Today, Lord, awaken me with a word for the weary. Counsel me with your words for those in need."

May the Lord use your tongue in ways that bring hope.

Love
Bec

NOTES

As I stood in a waiting room at the hospital, my heart was overwhelmed for each and every person in those seats... just waiting for what? Waiting for results? Waiting to go through a door to hope and peace? Would the wait end in bad reports? Fear? Unanswered questions? I hated the situations of each and every one. I hated that the room was full. I hated that they were hurting. I hated that I felt helpless to do anything, except smile and pray silently. As I drove home, I shared my feelings and was challenged by this question. What are you going to do about it? It was like an arrow to my heart. I hurt for those people and yet did nothing. Even now, I feel the tears welling in my eyes for them.

My question for myself and for you: what are you gonna do about the people and scenes before you? Just watch? Just walk away and do nothing? Forget them and move on? Our example is Jesus when the crowds were hungry. He challenged His disciples by asking them, "What are you going to do?" When they responded, "We have nothing much." Jesus said, "It just so happens you have a couple fish and a few loaves. That is enough.!" They had only a little, but God did a lot! They had more than enough to multiply. They had enough to take their faith to the next level and fuel a miracle.

They had more than enough in the hands of a mighty God. Has Jesus been asking you, "What are you going to do, friend?" Will you give God what you have? Are you willing to see the need and be moved to action?

Are you moved with compassion enough to step out?

Compassion isn't something we just put on; we move in it. How many times are we po-sitioned in the right place but do not take action? How do we go from talking to action?

We know the One who is the answer. When you think you can't, God is good at joining you in the place you step out in... He loves being the answer. He loves showing up. He loves that nothing is impossible. We don't have to be perfect— just simply trust when we step out in His Name.

For he knows our frame, he remembers that we are dust. Psalm 103:14

Let's make a commitment to live and believe His very Words and persist until we step into a miracle. Don't try to figure it all out. Don't look for a special formula. JUST BELIEVE! SEE the need, then step into position to bring the answer. The Bible tells us to lay hands on the sick and they will recover. Do you know someone sick today to put your hands on and pray? Deep down, I wouldn't want it any other way. I want to be a part of the awesomeness of what He can do this side of Heaven. Get excited! Pray! Step out in those places where you hate what is happening, and ask God to position you into a place of becoming part of the answer. I'm asking you as I was asked, What are you going to do about it?

Willing,

NOTES

_____

_____

_____

_____

_____

_____

_____

_____

_____

_____

_____

_____

_____

_____

_____

_____

_____

_____

_____

_____

_____

I remember that day so vividly. I still can feel tortured by what I could or should have done, instead of what I did.

Can you relate to those emotions? Do you have such a time that you "instant replay" in your mind? Multiple replays? These regrets only capture us in a space that keeps us from moving forward, hindering us from new experiences. They can also keep us from confidence, joy, peace, and rest. Regrets are to be given over to the One who can change the very course of history; the One that can do something when there is nothing in our own ability can or could do. Are you holding on to regrets you need to give of your loving Father who can make a beautiful thing out of them?

> *...To give them beauty for ashes, The oil of joy for mourning. Isaiah 61:3a*

Your ashes, your regrets, in the hand of the living God can become something so much more beautiful than what you could have pictured. Will you, friend, grab your ashes, hand them to the Lord and forgive yourself of your fallings? Many times I have brought before the Lord the day my husband Romaro died. I have experienced intense regret that I could have or should have done more. Perhaps I didn't fight hard enough. I didn't stand strong enough. Those thoughts can easily be on a replay loop. But I have learned to let Christ be all that He is, allow myself to be forgiven and freed from enslavement to the past. I am not afraid to tell God how I am feeling and ask Him where He was that day. I let go, knowing I don't carry power to change what happened, letting God know I trust Him as I walk free from being tied to that hospital room. I remind myself that I did all I knew to do and I did stand strong. I pray that you, too, will forgive yourself and actively confront thoughts of regret with thoughts of truth. Replace the lies of the enemy with Truth.

> *But one thing I do: forgetting what lies behind and straining forward to what lies ahead.*
> *Philippians 3:13*

The verse from the Apostle Paul carries much weight in light of his past. He did horrific things against Christ followers (Acts 8:1-3 & Acts 9:1-19). His life was full of actions that he could have looked back on with the deepest regret. He could have said, "I did too many things in my past." His guilt could have stopped him from living out the call of God on his life. That verse came alive in my heart once Romaro was gone. Was I going to live in a space full of regret or would I stop looking back and look forward to what Christ was going to do. Even if I didn't see my future, I declared Jeremiah 29:11 over and over:

> *For I know the thoughts that I think toward you, says the LORD, thoughts of peace and not of evil, to give you a future and a hope.*

No matter what your past carried, God is greater in your future.

There is hope and there is space for you to live free. My life, like Paul's can attest to that.

Forgetting the past, looking forward to the future,

Love

Rebecca

NOTES

_____

_____

_____

_____

_____

_____

_____

_____

_____

_____

_____

_____

_____

_____

_____

_____

_____

_____

Dear friend

How do you step into places you have never been? You have to be willing to step across the threshold of what makes sense and look beyond what seems normal or common. So many things that God asks us to do or places He calls us to, force us out of our comfort zone and into places of uncertainty; we can't see what it could turn out like. It makes us wonder, "Why this, Lord?" "Really?! You want me to do THAT?" I have watched many people turn back from God asking them to do something that we would consider ridiculous. When is the last time God asked you to do something that was ridiculous? Did you hear the Lord but chose natural reasoning over supernatural faith? Did you choose to lean on your own understanding? Have you chosen to stay where you are and not step through the passage into the unknown world of what God has planned for you?

I wonder if we counted, how many of the stories in the Bible have a mark of ridiculousness? How many could have reasoned it not to be of God? Do you hear God and then question, "that couldn't have been God"? If you follow a GPS, many times your own reasoning can come into play and you aren't willing to follow the device. Logic and common sense tell you that there's a shorter path or a better route. But God can see your destination. HE created that destination. He knows what will happen along the way too.

What's your passage? Are your feet at the threshold of something that you feel God is leading you into, but yet you won't step? We are all guilty of not stepping. Sometimes our lack of following has extreme consequences. There are times when there is more at risk than we can grasp; because of that, we can't lean into our own understanding. We have to trust that HE knows the end and the beginning. In those moments when our plans seem to be the most important or seem to make more sense, we have to check our plan at the door and pick up God's itinerary. His plan. His steps.

I know from experience, we don't get the total plan; the pieces and the steps just don't add up in our human minds. That should not stop us from following or trusting. If you knew the whole plan you wouldn't need God. Plus HE wants to do it with you.

Wherever His presence is, is where you want to be.

God isn't asking you to do what you know, because living by faith and not sight is stepping into His kingdom. There are places along the journey we have to jump. You have to trust your instruments. You have to know they will work. God has given you ALL you need for life and godliness.

His divine power has given us everything we need for a godly life through our knowledge of him who called us by his own glory and goodness. 2 Peter 1:3

It's more about who you are with, than what you do. If God has you, He has you. You can't live in the space that tends to lend to your human response. If You walk with him always thinking He won't show up, at some point you won't show up or you will just do it yourself. You have to cause your mind to truly believe that He is with you and willing. You can't live in the limbo; you can't walk with all the gear on and never jump. Jump. Jump! JUMP! It's scary, but in the end you won't regret it.

Blessings abound when we step out in faith. Live a life of faith!

Becca Love

NOTES

_____

_____

_____

_____

_____

_____

_____

_____

_____

_____

_____

_____

_____

_____

_____

_____

_____

What do you do when you have nothing to offer? Nothing left in your tank to give. Zero. And people are asking for more from you. Your job is calling, your children are calling, your parents are calling, your friends are blowing up your phone. This and that keep knocking. You are weary. You are at the end of your rope and feel like you are barely hanging on by a thread. Maybe today is your 23rd day in the hospital and you are wondering when, how and if it will ever change. Maybe you are done... with a capital D! Tonight, I feel overwhelmed, tired from a sleepless night, struggling with homeschooling my four kids, making some big decisions, and more! Yet, God tells me to get up and write. I had a one-sided conversation with the God of the universe: "Right now? Really? I'm tired!" He waited for me to realize that whenever I am at the end of my rope, the line is anchored in the very presence of God! When I think I have nothing to offer, God in me has more than enough to offer someone else through my seemingly empty vessel.

So many moments in the hospital with Romaro I was challenged by this verse:

He who refreshes others will be refreshed. Proverbs 11:25b

I went after it passionately. I was longing for someone to pour some courage into me. I was feeling sooo depleted. I leaned into that verse, asking God to prove it true in my life. Then I chose to look for places to refresh others. I looked for people in the midst of the battle so that I could encourage them. It was like I was taking it to the bank. If I needed encouragement, I gave it. Each time I would find a person to refresh, I knew somehow God would refresh me. That truth was beautiful, and so, so refreshing! There are times when we don't even see how much we need to be refreshed! Sometimes even when we are oblivious the kindness of God steps in and asks us to refresh someone else so that He can indeed refresh us.

Probably one of the biggest moments God stretched me in this truth was at my husband's funeral. The graveside service had just finished, his casket was still in my peripheral vision, when I felt the Lord's nudge to go to a couple and prophesy to them. I remember standing there, thinking, "Really Lord? Right now?" It was actually a divine set up for God to meet me; to do a work in my life by using me in someone else's life.

We tend to expect God to work within the world's frame. However, the world's frame and plan never consists of giving at the time of our greatest need. God says to **give** at our greatest moment of need, then He can fulfill his plan in and through us. God will never let His Word fall to the ground. When we have nothing, Christ can show up with everything! When we need strength, He becomes our strength. When we need wisdom, He is our wisdom. When we need counsel, He is the Wonderful Counselor. Christ can fill any place you feel depleted.

Refreshing others is right up my alley,

Love

Bec

NOTES

_____

_____

_____

_____

_____

_____

_____

_____

_____

_____

_____

_____

_____

_____

_____

_____

_____

_____

_____

dear friend

Grab your Bible and read Acts 10. As you read, listen for revelation from the Holy Spirit. I love that the Spirit can speak to us uniquely and differently as we read the same passage and meditate on it, using our individual experiences to bring new revelation.

Acts 10. Cornelius, a man of prestige, is seeking God, praying and doing charitable works for the Jewish people. He was a good man and because of his prayers, God stepped into his world, sent an angel to him and told him to invite Simon to his house. However, before Peter would be willing to meet with Cornelius, not a Jewish person, God used his hungry belly to change his thinking about non-Jewish people. God sent a vision of a sheet with certain animals on it and told him to eat, but Peter refused because he had been taught that these animals were not to be eaten by Jewish people. (Do we refuse God when He speaks because of what we have been taught or have as a preconceived idea of God?) God had to change Peter's mind, so when Peter kept refusing to listen, He repeated the vision to him three times. Once the sheet was taken back up into heaven, Peter was perplexed and trying to figure it out. God told him,

> *Some men are going to ask you to go visit a man. Go with them. As Peter went to Cornelius' home, he finally understood the vision. "God was telling me that whoever fears Him and does what is right, is acceptable to Him, no matter what people he belongs to.*
> *Acts 10:15*

The main idea Peter learned is that people are people and who God accepts into His kingdom is His decision. God was working with Simon Peter behind the scenes to orchestrate his plan for Cornelius and his household. Peter told Cornelius and all his family and friends about the love of God and recounted what Jesus had done for them. They all got saved, filled with the Spirit and baptized! Isn't that crazy amazing!?! God worked out the details because He is about the harvest of souls. He loves people, just like you and me. You never know who God will send to talk to you; or who He might send you to talk with. Let Him break down the barriers we might have set up in our minds so that we can be used like Cornelius and Peter to advance God's will and message of hope and salvation.

See what God is willing to do to make a way into our hearts.

Remember, your story is full of details and God IS working!

NOTES

So, in the middle of writing this devotional, I also started writing a fiction book. I know, I can't believe it either!

One day the thought of writing a fiction book crossed my mind, and I was like, "What if I tried?" I actually went to Google and searched, "how to write fiction." Google gave me a list of the top ten things. Yup, I started right there and followed them all... lol. Not really, but I did begin. The most interesting discovery was that I am supposed to "show" readers instead of "tell" readers what I want them to understand.

Maybe you already knew that, but, man, how valuable are those words!

Have you ever thought about what it would mean to show someone who God is instead of telling them; showing someone what God can do instead of telling them? The idea of "a story" was conceived.

God himself didn't come on the scene and tell us He was the creator of the World; He actually opened up the scene and showed us all the things He created.

And God said, "Let there be light," and there was light. And God saw that the light was good. And God separated the light from the darkness. God called the light Day, and the darkness he called Night. And there was evening and there was morning, the first day. Genesis 1:3-5

The Lord God took the man and put him in the garden of Eden to work it and keep it. Genesis 2:15

Then He showed us how he would save the world, instead of announcing it from the Heavens:

But when they came to Jesus and saw that he was already dead, they did not break his legs. But one of the soldiers pierced his side with a spear, and at once there came out blood and water. He who saw it has borne witness— his testimony is true, and he knows that he is telling the truth— that you also may believe. John 19:33-35

He showed us how he cared for us, through stories and people. Read Mark 8:1-10. We are so used to the idea of walking around and telling people of God's love that we often overlook that God asked us to show His love. Love people. Don't just tell people. Matthew 22:37-40 says:

And he said to him, "You shall love the Lord your God with all your heart and with all your soul and with all your mind. This is the great and first commandment. And a second is like it: You shall love your neighbor as yourself.

Let actions speak louder than words.

In your story, What are you doing to show God's love? The Bible lists things we can do as an expression of our love:

"Feed the hungry" (Psalm 146:7)

"Heal the sick" (Matthew 10:8)

"Take care of the orphans" (Psalm 146:9

"Set the captives free" (Isaiah 61:1)

"Take care of widows" (Psalm 146:9)

"Love your neighbor" (Matthew 19:19)

"Bring justice to the oppressed" (Ps. 146:7)

"Pray for your enemies" (Matthew 5:44)

In Luke 5:20-26 is a story about Jesus healing a man. Notice the difference between telling someone, "You can be forgiven" and "You are forgiven." Jesus showed the man forgiveness through healing. Aren't you glad God didn't just say it, but actually showed us His great unsearchable love?! He stepped down from His high position in Heaven to come to earth to show us His love. He showed us everything that He could have just told us. I am forever grateful!

Determined to show more than tell,

NOTES

_____

_____

_____

_____

_____

_____

_____

_____

_____

Nothing wasted. We live in a country where so much is wasted. We waste food, the bit left in a bottle, the cold coffee left in a mug, etc. I feel such a pressing need to NOT waste. It's not just about food...I don't want to waste time, creativity, strength, love or even a conversation because God doesn't waste anything. He didn't waste time, words in the Bible, his strength...nothing!

Each thing that is in your story is there on purpose.

It's easy to focus on the highlight reels, but what about looking at the experiences, ideas, thoughts, actions, even people might simply ignore.

What do you toss aside, that could be more important than you give it credit for? What ideas are deleted? Have you ever considered that the things most people could or would pass up, might be just the right ones? What if an idea that ends up in the trash was the step to a larger one? I'm asking you to consider the potential purpose of wasted ideas; the passageway between one significant thing to another. Small moments add up to be more of our life than the big, significant moments.

Consider the seemingly insignificant moments like doing the dishes, picking up your kids, brushing teeth, folding laundry...all the time that is in the mundane, the quiet, the routine, the boring, the normal...what if for one day you didn't waste that moment? What if you chose to make that activity special and meaningful? For example, when you do the dishes you could try any of the following: pray for a specific person or place, put music on and make it a dance party or a worship session, intentionally make the water more bubbly and share the bubbles, ask if you can do the dishes for someone else, or have the Bible App read to you. Make the mundane full of intention!

Pay attention to those moments you wish you could skip past; they could become some of your best moments if you don't view them as wasted time. I'm not saying take every moment and make it loud or change the culture of it, but might we be more intentional in not wasting it. Not just to fill it, but seek God and ask Him how to not waste moments and times He has graciously given you to love, care, listen, and be faithful with.

Read Luke 10:38-42. What's your take away from it?

It's easy to be distracted in what we are doing, without being focused on what we could be doing.

Determined to stop waste,

NOTES

dear friend

How do you express your love? Ever feel that your love is not enough for those in your life? Ever think, "I wish I could love them better? What if I work on this or that…?"

It would be great if we were able to give all the love someone else needed; if we had a well of love that was just right. Wouldn't the world be an amazing place to live if we all loved perfectly?

I used to think just that. I lived a long time always feeling bad about myself when I wasn't able to fill the love tank of my husband or my children just so. As much as I wanted to have enough for everyone, I didn't. Sometimes I didn't even want to do all the things they expected of me (the guilt of not wanting to do it was real, too.) I struggled with my insufficiency and felt like I wasn't being a good enough wife or mother.

But that idea was challenged by this idea: Growth doesn't always come from my conforming to what a person thinks he/she needs from me. Sometimes "real and raw love" is what they actually need for fulfillment and growth. Love is still present, even when we aren't demonstrating it in exactly the form that someone else is expecting.

God's love for us is never absent, even when He goes against what we think is normal or it isn't looking the way we think it should.

Let's look at the story of Lazurus in John 11:1-44. Jesus' love wasn't evident as the story was unfolding. God was working the entire time even when it didn't seem like He was. He was waiting for the perfect moment to display His love at an even a greater degree than they were asking. Mary and Martha wanted Jesus to heal their brother, but Jesus disappointed them (did not show his love the way they wanted or expected). Instead he showed His love for them with an even greater miracle than defeating sickness—He defeated death! With them, we finally see that His love was visible in the waiting, in the lack, in the unknown. He showed them a new expression of love.

In the days ahead when they were in the waiting period between the cross and the resurrection, they could have the confidence in the power of God's love. Their experience in the waiting, the disappointment, had shown how willing and able God was to raise Lazarus from the dead. Even death wasn't strong in the light of God's love.

God's plan and love was richer than they had experienced before. The love caused them to grow a new level of trust. This love wasn't pretty and sweet in the moment, but raw and real, tough and willing to push back all the pain they were feeling. Jesus showed us a love that was selfless. He actually felt their feelings, but God loved them enough to not fill the small needs because He knew they would need more.

Loving them differently gave way for them to grow.

(However, this was not an excuse for me not to lean into what doesn't come easy… like physical touch for example; often we are pushed out of our comfort zone in showing love in ways that don't come naturally for us).

What a release of pressure to know that the gap can be a place of growth, instead of an indication of the absence of God's love. God's love for us is never absent, even when He goes against what we think should be or isn't looking the way we expected. God's love fills every gap.

We, as humans, are not meant to completely fulfill or satisfy our loved ones... that's God's job. Only God can love our family and friends perfectly, in all the ways we can't. Can you see the love of God in the gaps when you don't see or feel His love? You know He doesn't set love aside. He truly loves you, even when it comes in a different package than you expect.

Believing "how" He loves me is best,

NOTES

_____

_____

_____

_____

_____

_____

_____

_____

_____

_____

_____

_____

_____

_____

Have you looked in the mirror today?

What catches your attention? Why did you look?

The purpose of looking in the mirror is to see what we can't see.

That reflection gives us a new perspective.

I started thinking about how we can look to the Father in order to reflect Him. Do I come to the Word of God to change my reflection? Do I bask in the Word to be more like Him? God has a character and Spirit we can reflect. As we read the Word intentionally, we can see examples of how Jesus reflected his Father in all aspects of his ministry and daily life. The Word reveals clarity, help, and purpose.

As I have been writing, I've been thinking about the ways to do it; how to put words into sentences; how to make it impactful. I have struggled in writing. Okay to be honest, I see all my inabilities, my mistakes, my bad grammar. I can see all of that. But I felt like God was calling me, so how do I lean in, when I don't know how? That's when it dawned on me that God is an Author!

Most people told me to read, look at authors and see how they write; telling me to be intentional in reading. I started to read the Bible, with the intent of seeing Him as an Author— the First Author. I wanted to learn from God, the greatest author of all time!

The journey has been interesting. I see the stories differently...I see the points of his creative authoring. I began to see the Author I wanted to reflect...I turned to the author of the best selling book of all time to better reflect His writing technique. I want to be able to reflect Him in and through my authoring. It has been easier for me to approach the uncomfortable places of my life as an author, looking for a kingdom message, knowing I have the greatest example to follow, One who wants to help me. There is something comforting about knowing He already has done what I am doing.

Today I read the parable of the sower (Matthew 13:10-16) and noticed Jesus' creativity and style as he's telling the story. He was showing his audience the story, not just telling them. Jesus secretly added the mysteries of the kingdom within the script and dialogue. I see that as He wrote, He kept the important things and cut the fat.

God's Word gives us so many great examples: how to's and even mysteries of the kingdom. Take a week, as you read the Bible, and look intentionally to see God/Jesus doing whatever you do...how is He a businessman? How is He a parent? How is He artistic? How does He sing and make music?

If you are a business man/woman, notice what God says about business. If you are homeschooling, look for examples of how Jesus taught. If you are in customer service, observe how Jesus dealt with the public. If you are in a trade, watch what kind of a carpenter He was. Do this for anything you do or are into. Reflect on how He functioned in the gift or profession, notice his quiet times and the times He boldly cried out. Notice His rhythm. See if you can find something about Him that could change your walk to reflect him more. James 1:22-24 tells us:

But be doers of the word, and not hearers only, deceiving yourselves. For if anyone is a hearer of the word and not a doer, he is like a man who looks intently at his natural face in a mirror. For he looks at himself and goes away and at once forgets what he was like.

Look intently into the Word, like you are looking for more clarity, help and purpose today in whatever you are called to do.

Bringing back the reflection,

Love

Rebecca

NOTES

_____

_____

_____

_____

_____

_____

_____

_____

_____

_____

_____

_____

_____

You are not alone.

You might feel alone. Your circumstances might have left you alone. You might be crying yourself to sleep because you are so lonely. Yet, you are not alone.

You are NOT alone.

God declares in His Word, that He will never leave you nor forsake you (Hebrews 13:5).

The Great I AM is with you.

If today you find yourself in the first few sentences, my heart aches for you. God didn't create you to be alone. Recently, I found myself with a few friends at different times who all expressed to me that they felt so alone.

I wonder about you. About your best friend. About your family. Are you one of those people surrounded by others, hundreds of friends on facebook and yet wallowing in a state of loneliness? How many times I have felt alone after Rome passed away! He was my very best friend, and it totally was lonely not to speak to him anymore. People that loved me surrounded me, but I was looking for someone who wasn't there. Maybe that's you.

During that time, God taught me that even if I wasn't looking for him, it didn't mean He wasn't there. If I wasn't speaking to Him, it didn't mean He wasn't speaking to me. Maybe my ears were just listening to all the spaces of emptiness I was experiencing. God hasn't ever left me, nor you.

Joseph (Genesis 37-43) had an experience where he probably felt alone. He was ripped from what he knew. His brothers hated him. His father never came looking for him (he was told he was dead). He was a slave. He was lied about. He was falsely accused. He was locked up. He was forgotten. (Hopefully not all those things have happened to you.)

In this painful scenario, it seemed like all the odds were stacked against him; that life was unfair and he was trapped in a circle of being alone, and forgotten. It would be so easy to think, "Where are you God?" Did God totally forget about him? It just so happens in Psalm 105:17-19, we get to see the truth of what was really happening in Joseph's life:

He sent a man ahead of them, Joseph, who was sold as a slave. His feet were hurt with fetters; his neck was put in a collar of iron; until what he had said came to pass, the word of the Lord tested him.

Joseph was sent. He was the answer to a future problem only God knew about. He was never alone. He was commissioned. It just didn't look like what he or I would have pictured for someone's life. God knew. He knew what was coming, and He knew He needed someone to be the answer.

We can't look at all the lonely space, the unknown space, the unwanted space, the feared space... and say God isn't there. We have to look through the space and see God, and who He is and what He can do.

Friend, you are not alone. You are called. Just don't get your picture of what the answer will look like confused with what God's picture looks like. Learn to trust God in the lonely. In the uncomfortable. In the waiting. In the silence. In the loss. In the pain. In each and everything you could add to that list.

If I have learned anything in the past 6 years, it is that no matter what the circumstances, God is there. How He shows up just might not be what I was hoping He would show up like. Yet even so, He was there. He is ALWAYS with me and I am NEVER alone.

You are NEVER alone,

Beccafore

NOTES

_____

_____

_____

_____

_____

_____

_____

_____

_____

dear friend

Today, I was given the opportunity to step through a door that was so hard. Standing in front of those doors, all I wanted to do was run. I didn't want to be there. I didn't want to walk with my friend to the room where we would wait for her appointment with her blood doctor. The same waiting room I had waited in with Romaro many times. I hated the thought of being there.

I had a talk with myself—do I run from those kinds of moments and say," it's just too hard?" Do I stand and see all the giants in the land? Do I see pain and hurt hovering? Do I let all the feelings and past experiences keep me from moving into breakthrough, or into the promises God has purchased for me? After Romaro died, I made the decision that no door, place, or memory was gonna hold me back from being with someone who needed me.

I remembered back to the 1st anniversary of Romaro's passing. That day, I chose to walk through the threshold of the hospital where Romaro had passed away; through those doors that once closed behind me when I felt only defeat. But on the anniversary, I couldn't believe I was standing there willing to push open the door by faith with peace and victory. Dang, it was hard. I walked every inch of that hallway to take back every moment I agonized up and down them a year ago. I refused to let the enemy come up with any place that I was not willing to conquer.

The hospital doors behind which Romaro passed away were nothing but doors, after all. And doors open. God has opened doors for me before and has always walked through them with me. Am I willing to walk into the unknown with the God who is faithful?

I thought of Joshua who walked into the promised land 40 years before he ended up going in permanently. He was one of the two willing to step across into the unknown, with little to lose as he surveyed the land. It just so happens, 40 years later, God brought him back to the exact same place and asked even more: "Will you lead my people? Will you go and conquer? Will you be courageous?" If God asked Joshua to not be afraid, then it means that he totally was afraid!! Yet he still stepped into that land of giants.

My takeaway?

When life takes you back through the same door, don't hesitate. Walk boldly. Walk with confidence.

Time can sometimes be our biggest excuse for not moving forward. Have you ever stood on the top of an obstacle and hesitated for a second. How long did that second last? You can't let your seconds of hesitation turn into you turning around! God wants us to step through doors into every promise He has purchased for us.

Friend, you will see the power of the living God, if you just don't hesitate. Fear stopped all those people from going into the promised land. Fear can be present, but you can walk fearlessly when you choose to walk hand in hand with the living God. Take His hand, walk closely, and listen well. He will lead you into the most amazing spaces even if it requires more courage than you think you have. In those places, you will find freedom where you once were enslaved.

Never gonna hesitate,

Relena Gore

NOTES

_____

_____

_____

_____

_____

_____

_____

_____

_____

_____

_____

_____

_____

_____

_____

_____

I'm sitting at a coffee shop in Waco, TX thinking about how I could encourage you. Wondering how life has been going, and how big your struggles are. My heart longs to encourage you today to STEP OUT!

Step out of your comfortable. Step into BOLD.

Perhaps you have been hurt before by stepping out. Maybe you would tell me that you got burned when you stepped out. Maybe, on the other side of the coffee table, you would share with me whatever didn't work, how great the loss was, or how embarrassed you felt.

Whatever you would tell me, I would tell you it again (within reason): Keep stepping out!

If you write, *write boldly.*

If you sing, *create a new song.*

If you dance, *bust a new move.*

If you adventure, *go to a new level.*

If you wanna do something no one has ever done, *you have to step somewhere no one has ever been.*

Go! Even if you are in unknown territory. You are on common ground with everyone who went before you. (It just so happens that I am sitting in Common Grounds coffee shop.) You, me and many that have come before us, and many that will come after us, stand on the same ground. Some have been ready, but possibly not really willing to move. Please friend, don't hold back.

Seriously, you do not have to have all the answers. You don't have to know the way. You just have to have courage to begin. You have to be willing to step outside of your normal, and find where God is. He steps in and shows up.

Oh wait, maybe you could look me straight in the eyes and say, that won't happen. I get it, for real. Perhaps your journey hasn't come to the place where it collides with what God only can do.Those divine moments of the hand of God in our lives are amazing. Don't back away from the endless possibilities. Don't let your comfy pants, house, job, security, etc. hold you as a slave. A world is waiting for you to become what God created you to be.

Think about Abram who was literally told to "Go." Not the entire plan, only that the future would be good. (Genesis 12:1-3). God tells us the same:

For I know the plans I have for you, declares the Lord, plans for welfare and not for evil, to give you a future and a hope. Jeremiah 29:11

God spoke what Abram was to do— obey and go. He had a choice, though, just like you do. His journey wasn't without unknowns and hard places. Yet, God was there. I'm just asking, if God says "Go," are you willing?

What has God been saying to you? Write it down, even if it sounds a little crazy.

How long have you waited to take the first step? Abram took that first step, as many others, and I have done before you. We are all on common ground, go outside and put your feet in the grass... same grass as me. Step boldly and go.

Taking first steps,

Becca

NOTES

_____

_____

_____

_____

_____

_____

_____

_____

_____

_____

_____

_____

_____

_____

dear friend

Let's start off by reading 2 Kings 4:38-41. I wondered why we needed to know that there was a famine in the land? Why did God tell us that? It sets the stage —famine means there was a lack; people were desperate for food. The lack was real and people had to deal with what was happening in their world. It creates an understanding of people being desperate.

In this episode, it was soup night at the prophet's house. Elijah had asked for soup for all, so the servant went looking for food in the wild because no one had food (famine, remember?) The servant found some likely looking vegetables growing on a vine, so he picked a bunch of it, brought it back to Elijah's place, and made soup out of his find.

Have you ever made a meal and it made your guests sick? (If you have, please don't invite me over, LOL. I haven't, so I think you would be safe to come to my house.)

This day, the Bible recounts, the soup didn't just make them sick but would have caused people to die. Literally. The things picked in the field for the soup were poisonous (my footnote says they were probably poisonous mushrooms that the servant found growing). BTW- these were not his enemies but his boys; his friends.

I loved Elisha's response—he asked for flour, threw it in the pot, and solved the problem. I don't understand how the flour resolved the death in the soup—it's a mystery miracle. But it worked because the soup then was served to the men, they ate it, and didn't die. Maybe keep spare flour with you, or when you visit someone, idk. :)

The miracle was awesome, but that isn't the point. Look at how he responded. Elisha didn't freak out. The people around him were freaking out—death was in their bowls. They were panicking. Seriously, who wouldn't? These were men of faith, too (prophets). Yet only Elisha paused and responded. He remained in peace. Pay attention to that fact—**no matter what is happening, God responds from a place of peace.** He is the Prince of Peace.

How do we remain in a place of peace instead of allowing the trouble of the earth to trouble us?

1. God wants us to trust him in all circumstances.

2. Knowing our kingdom rights. Romans 14:17 says peace is ⅓ of the kingdom.

3. Positioning oneself in peace. Refuse to freak out like everyone else. God wants us to live above the situation and bring His peace into it. Let God actually be the peace in our heart and mind. We can carry peace into the situation and be the one to seek God. Miracles are on the other side of your difficulty. Miracles are in the places we can't control. Know that God is in control and can move in and through our peace.

· · ·

How do you bring peace? Declare it. Isaiah 57:19

Pause and think through all the impossible things God could do. Stop thinking through all the possibilities of what could happen.

Let your mind and heart know who (REALLY) is in control. (Proverbs 19:21)

Know God can and will work things out. Romans 8:28

Pray and meditate on this scripture until it changes the atmosphere to peace:

Do not be anxious about anything, but in everything by prayer and supplication with thanksgiving let your requests be made known to God. And the PEACE of God, which surpasses ALL your understanding, will guard your hearts and your minds in Christ Jesus. Philippians 4:6

I speak the SHALOM Peace of God over you.

Nothing missing, nothing broken.

NOTES

_____

_____

_____

_____

_____

_____

_____

_____

Today IS A GOOD DAY!

Say that outloud this time.

Today (while I'm sitting at the dentist office) is the day the Lord has made (Psalm 118:24). Take a second, and rejoice in this day. If you paused, and thought only of all things that you don't know about today, all the things that aren't gonna be good, STOP it! Stop, pause for the next few minutes and surrender those thoughts to how good God is. Realize He has been with you so far today and He will be with you the rest of today.

THEN… Recognize that in one moment things can change.

You can go from hungry to full in a moment. You can go from needing money to a full bank account in a moment. You can go from not having a child to having one in a moment. You can go from no job, to a job in a moment. You can go from Miss to Mrs. in a moment. You can go from sick to well in a moment.

In ONE moment, God can shift everything. Why not expect it to shift for the good? Personally, I can see the glass half empty. God started checking me on this. (Have you ever had God check you on something??) My focus needed to change, so I began to remind myself God is for me and not against me. Once I started looking at everything with fresh eyes, renewed hope, expectation, and excitement it changed my negatives to joy, peace and patience in the midst of the trials.

Psalm 23:5 speaks of the table in the presence of our enemies. That doesn't mean that the enemies went "POOF" and disappeared. Gone. Adios. No, it just meant in the midst of chaos, when I can hear my enemy, in the heat of the circumstance, I can sit with God, and calmly eat a GIANT BURRITO, aka, good meal. As I sit at the table, they can surround me, but I do not have to fear, be worried or overwhelmed! I can enjoy the presence of the Father and the knowledge that He is around, and everything is alright.

Today is a good day because and only because God made today and God is good.
Nothing can separate God and good. Today we can declare:

God is for me.

Today is good.

Today is full of God's provision.

Today is full of Peace.

My life will be full of Hope.

I'm going to enjoy today with God.

I will not fear.

I will not worry.

I will trust God.

He is NOT against me.

Today is going to be AWESOME!

Part of David's story is written for us in 1 Samuel 30. His enemy came in when he was gone and took everything! His stuff, kids, wife and all of his people's stuff and families. Can you imagine walking next to everything that was raided, everything turned over, and nothing left? He was left devastated and drained. And then everything went from bad to worse: his closest friends and followers wanted to kill him. Instead of looking at the devastation and betrayal, David stepped away and we read that He encouraged himself in the Lord (Samuel 30:6). David paused in the moment and sought the Lord.

One moment... everything was lost.

Yet, after one moment with God and using His strategy, everything was completely recovered. EVERYTHING. Reread 1 Samuel 30:18-20. God redeemed everything for him, and redeeming it not only affected him, but also his friends and men, his and their wives and children. Encouraging yourself in the Lord, and obeying God affects your family, your friends, your coworkers, and your world just like it did for David.

Much love and joy, encouraging myself in the Lord,

Love
Rebeca

NOTES

_____

_____

_____

_____

_____

_____

 Dear friend

How's your day? I woke up yesterday and wished that it was over before it began. It was "that kind of day." I thought about all "that day" had in store and I didn't even want to live it. I expected a horrible day! What do you do when your calendar turns into "that day?" When was the last time you felt like that? What day was it?

The time went slowly, the seconds seemed like hours. For much of "that day," I prayed and prayed (1 Peter 5:7). As the day came to a close, all the hard places had been hard, but not crazy hard like I had imagined they would be. My heart finally began to calm. I sat on my bed and processed "that day." I thought about what I could have accomplished and done if I wouldn't have been worrying and stressing over all the what if's.

I sat there and repented over my lack of trust and fear. Truth is, those days come, so what do we do with them? Do we let them rule us or do we rule that day? Where do we turn? Jesus encountered a time when he awoke with the pressures all around him on "that day."

On that day, when evening had come, he said to them, "Let us go across to the other side." And leaving the crowd, they took him with them in the boat, just as he was. And other boats were with him. And a great windstorm arose, and the waves were breaking into the boat, so that the boat was already filling.

*But he was in the stern, asleep on the cushion. And they woke him and said to him, "Teacher, do you not care that we are perishing?" And he awoke and rebuked the wind and said to the sea, **"Peace! Be still!"** And the wind ceased, and there was a great calm. He said to them, "Why are you so afraid? Have you still no faith?" And they were filled with great fear and said to one another, "Who then is this, that even the wind and the sea obey him?" Mark 4:35-41*

Most of the time, when those days come, a week later you can't even remember all that happened. When "that day" hits, what could you do to not let it affect your whole day?

First, pause and take a few deep breaths.

Next, find a Scripture that encourages you, write it on a card and put it in your pocket. When your heart gets all crazy, read the Word.

OK. This is even easier. Friend, can you remember these three words— Peace! Be still! Just like what Jesus said. Peace. Be still.

He woke up to a storm around Him.

Chaos surrounded Him and He just spoke to it, saying three simple and powerful words: Peace. Be Still.

Your heart can be stilled just like waves. Rebuke the chaos and let Christ fill your mind and heart. Focus your faith on God's ability to rule over whatever the chaos is. Do you rule the time of each moment or do those things control you? Do you let faith or fear have your time? I know it isn't easy, but learn that your circumstances do not reign, God does.

Peace, be still! John 14:27

NOTES

_____

_____

_____

_____

_____

_____

_____

_____

_____

_____

_____

_____

_____

_____

_____

_____

Dear friend

Check out Hagar in Genesis 16. Read her story, her hurt, the unfairness of the problem, and/or her brokenness. Do you see yourself in her story? Think about the places in your story where you feel broken or abandoned. Possibly you have places of distress, regret, unfixable situations... places you wish you could just tell someone about but there isn't anyone to listen. Please, know that God hears you! Just start speaking to Him about those deep places, the hurts, your fears, your mistakes, even those places of doubt and struggle. God, the One who is outrageously huge, has it! He is jealous, wanting all of you.

The Spirit that God breathed in our hearts is a jealous lover who intensely desires to have more and more of us. James 4:5

You know those places you wouldn't want anyone to even know about... He wants them and you intensely. Before you breathed, He knew each and everything that would happen and all you would or wouldn't do. He actually chose to go before you and stay on the cross to pay the full amount just to have the "chance" of having your heart. You were given a choice even though the price was paid. He unlocked the door of the prison of your brokenness. You just have to open the door. He left you with the power to choose. How much access will you allow Him? How much freedom will you step into? Those broken places, unfixable situations, unknowns... those are all places where you have to invite Him into. He can change them around, when you allow Him the freedom to do so.

Sometimes we don't ask because we truly don't know God like that. If you only know God as Savior, when you are sick you would never go to Him. You would try everyone and everything else but not our Great Physician. Yet, it is the one place that healing comes from. God is a healer. Psalm 103:2-3

Pause again.

Ask God to make Himself known to you in that place of unrest you were thinking about earlier. For instance, until Romaro was gone, I never went to God as my husband. I knew He could be but I just trusted in what my eyes, hands, and heart knew in front of me. I knew Romaro to be my husband, and he was what I knew.

When I became a widow, everything changed. **I had to press into God differently.** Psalm 68:5 calls God "Husband to the widow," but reading that wasn't enough. Experiencing and knowing Him is far more rich than just a title. I got to actually see Him show up for me in places that were difficult— my broken places, my decision making. God as my husband changed my life. He fixed the unfixable. He covered my butt sometimes. I needed help so much, friend.

Let God make Himself known to you... let Him be for you what you need.

Ask God who He is in your day? Ask Him to make Himself known to you. God sees you, just like He saw Hagar.

So she called the name of the Lord who spoke to her, "You are a God of seeing," for she said, "Truly here I have seen him who looks after me." Genesis 16:13

God sees you, sweet friend. He invested in the relationship with you already by the blood of His son, Jesus. He is available, gracious and compassionate. He longs to step into your space with all of Himself to be just what you need. He loves helping you.

Don't fear.

Trust God.

He loves you.

God sees me, and you, too,

NOTES

dear friend

Starbucks it is today! Hopefully this passion tea I'm drinking will bring out my passion, lol. I hope today speaks to you and encourages you in a secret place.

Do you have a secret world of disappointment?

Are there check marks on your door of how many times you have been disappointed? Do you keep a log of how many people have let you down? Does disappointment hinder your faith?

Now get real... What's your greatest disappointment? Your longest unanswered prayer? When faith pops up into your heart, do you crush it with, "Is that even possible?"

Have you stopped believing, friend?

Please consider that disappointment doesn't protect your heart.

Disappointment ends up stunting hearts and shutting out possibilities. So how can we trust God in disappointment?

One of the biggest ways we can trust God is to recognize that we can't see the full picture. We legit can't see all the places in which God is working. (Rereading the last sentence, I remind myself, in this difficult moment, to keep believing God is working even if I can't see it.) God can and has taken the perceived bad in my life and made it good (Romans 8:28). Please friend, don't let your narrow view of time lead you down a road of disappointment.

My Romans 8:28 experience just so happened when God spoke to me that He had a house for me and my children. The story seems simple. God spoke it and it happened. Yes. But all the middle was long, tiring, frustrating, exciting and disappointing. We looked at so many homes, tried to buy a few and yet no house for us. We looked for 2 years. I found myself saying, "Really God?" We actually had an offer on one and everything that could stop it from being ours, happened. I even considered I was in the wrong place. There were many moments, I really thought I was wrong. Yet, His timing was everything! And in the waiting God was working. It was invisible work, yet He was working.

Are you willing to stay trusting God, even when all the odds seem to be stacked against you? Are you willing to wait for the faithfulness of God to be displayed on your behalf, even if it takes years? Or will you walk away in the middle? Will you stop instead of moving forward? Are you trusting in today's experience rather than God's promise that hasn't manifested yet?

Friend, today call your disappointment out on the carpet. Name it and shame it! (LOL! I don't know where that came from, but it made me laugh.) Check out Mary's disappointment:

When Mary reached the place where Jesus was and saw him, she fell at his feet and said,
"Lord, if you had been here, my brother would not have died." John 11:32

God was doing something way bigger than Mary even dreamed. Jesus wasn't swayed by their momentary feelings (disappointments) because He knew they would compare to the magnitude of God's glory about to be revealed. HE was working when Mary didn't see what He was really doing.

Your situation is not hidden to Him. He sees just where you are. Possibly we can't see the greatness of what God is doing, because we don't have the full picture.

Let's not let our temporary disappointment get in the way of what God is doing. We can't let disappointment build a wall around us, keeping us from receiving what God has for us. Instead of giving in to disappointments, let's trust He is doing something wonderful for our good and His glory.

God understands the waiting. He isn't unaware of your hurt. Your pain. Your feelings. Your frustrations. In fact, in this story, Jesus wept with them before the miracle (John 11:35). When we are feeling unsure, take it to Jesus and then listen. Mary's vision wasn't big enough to imagine the answer to her prayer for her brother because it was bigger than she expected. Ask God for a greater understanding and faith that He is working on your behalf. Their story illustrates the fact that God has the power not only to heal, but to resurrect the dead.

What will you do when those chains of disappointment linger?

Break it off, so you can be free to see all God is doing. Be like Mary and Martha... ask Jesus and wait for his answer.

Praying for you tonight.

NOTES

_____

_____

_____

_____

_____

_____

Does your email box have little notification circle that cries for your attention? Is it over 100? 1000? Mine is currently 136 on my computer.

My phone doesn't have even one little circle...it just bings for my attention.

Some people aren't bothered with a notification or not. I personally don't like the circle.

Just curious... who can notify you and you respond to immediately?

Who do you sometimes respond to without thought?

How about this, who is it that you are waiting for the sound of the BING to happen? You know, when you look at your phone 5 or 6 times, hoping to see at least that they have read your last message, or there is a little dot dot dot... just to know they are typing. You check to make sure your ringer is on and you didn't even hear anything. Who is it???

The Bible is full of notifications: pray(bing!), love(bing!), serve(bing!), do not fear (bing!), be compassionate(bing!), be reasonable(bing!), be gracious(bing!), be courageous(bing!), wait for me(bing!), follow me(bing!), die to flesh(bing!), etc...

As you read them, do we let them slip by and become a number... not having time for it, ignoring it, or unaware of what it's trying to say to us?

God wants to reach us, to have conversation, do life with us (Romans 6:8).

Communication, in relationships, is the main idea. It's the reason that Jesus set up a plan, long before you existed, just for conversation with you. Do you sit and have conversations with Him? Do you think it is even possible?

In the old Testament, God spoke to Abraham. Abraham was called and chosen by God. God made Himself known to Abraham. They talked back and forth. What do you think it sounded like, looked like, or felt like? Could others hear them talk back and forth or did he just have to explain what it was like? The scripture records the conversations they had together, like in Genesis 18:22-33. We might say, of course God spoke to Him. He was a "man," chosen, loved, called, righteous, etc. As Abraham's story continues, we find that Hagar, a slave woman from Egypt, becomes intertwined in his story. She was aware of the times God spoke to Abraham. The mystery, the wildness of it, how rare it was. She heard the stories of all God had done on his behalf. One day, Hagar, without her consent, became the answer to what Abraham and his wife thought would fulfill the promise of God. She bore a son for Abraham.

Read the next part of her story in Genesis 16:7-14. Everything went south and she was banished, scared and afraid. In the middle of her running, God was there.

He knew right where she was, and He SPOKE to her.

God had a conversation with this slave. He spoke to her like He spoke to Abraham.

I love that God spoke to her. He doesn't pay attention to our rank. He loves each one of us, exactly where we are. His plan is that we can have a conversation with Him. We don't have to pretend, or try or have just the right things to say. He just wants to talk. (BING!) The Bible will show you, time and time again, God keeps speaking to us. He has never hung up, or blocked your text. Lol.

Respond to the One speaking to you from the Bible. Just start talking. Pour out your day to Him. Tell Him what you are excited about. Tell Him your good news, and bad news. Let Him into your decisions. He's waiting for your response so He can have a conversation with you. Just in case you want to tell me that is Old Testament and doesn't apply to today, John wrote in the New Testament:

To him the gatekeeper opens. The sheep hear his voice, and he calls his own sheep by name and leads them out. When he has brought out all his own, he goes before them, and the sheep follow him, for they know his voice. John 10:3-4

Jesus told us that His sheep will know His voice. Doesn't that mean He is talking to you?

What is God saying to you?

NOTES

_____

_____

_____

_____

_____

_____

_____

_____

I encourage you to consider something new.

What was the last thing you bought? A new scented candle, a new car, a new couch, or that new experience with a new food at a new restaurant?

Did any of those awesome things begin with someone challenging you or pushing you out of your normal, comfortable rhythm?

Recently, I was talking with someone who has known me most of my life, and she said something about me... and I was a little taken back. I thought, "I'm not that person anymore." I wanted to tell her, "Don't you know me? Can't you tell I have grown?" Friend, don't let people hold you back. Don't let them box you into who you used to be when you are not the same. Sometimes, people just say dumb things... they literally don't think. Remember that. (That's some good advice, lol).

Once Romaro and I went to a little brick oven pizza place he found from a TV show. (It's in the twin cities: Lola's Pizza.) I'm normally a pepperoni girl; I order the same thing every time. Then the server came and told us about the daily special. The toppings intrigued me so I ordered it. Romaro looked at me like I had just gone crazy... he was in shock. This was completely out of character for me.

The pizza was sooooo good (and that's an understandment)! Romaro described it as, "a rainbow of favors in your mouth." Years later, I still talk about it. That's just one small story in my life... a moment when I stepped outside of my box. When I decided that the boundaries I had put on myself weren't going to limit me.

Truthfully, I am normally very consistent. When I go to Starbucks I order a Peppermint mocha 90% of the time. I don't tend to try new things. I get the same drink every time... for 10 years straight! But I tried a Chai once, and now I get that too!! :) Habit is part of the awesomeness of who I am, yet I always want to grow. Recently, I was invited by a friend to play basketball, and then soccer. I've played basketball before, but not soccer. Soccer was a big step outside of my comfort zone and I am so glad I took that step. I have met some amazing people outside of my box.

I want to encourage you today to step outside of your normal. If you get invited to try something new...step out and say YES!! If you are sitting outside a place before going into somewhere new, listening to your inside voice saying, "This is too different, too crazy, too much," that was me, sitting in a different car in a different parking lot. But, man, I'm glad I didn't reverse the car and leave. My new experience, new friends, and new revelations about myself have been worth those few uncomfortable moments of panic.

Basketball has been more than to me than making baskets, getting rebounds. I'm creating relationships, receiving encouragement from others, developing courage, laughing more, nursing a black eye... (lol). All that is worth so much more than my pride.

Soccer has been so much more than my feet doing all the tricks, or getting a head bump. Not only have I gained new skills and focus on something totally out of my normal, I've met people I wouldn't ever have met otherwise. I've laughed a lot while playing too.

I was thinking about how, if in our normal temporal things, we are not willing to step out of our comfort zone, how are we going to step out of our spiritual comfort zones? Are we willing to advance in our spiritual walks by taking risks and doing the uncomfortable?

God always wants to draw us out. Before Peter walked on the water with Jesus, he asked for an invitation. "Jesus if you are there, call me out there with you. " (Matthew 14:28) What a good idea! If Jesus invites me into a new place, I know God has me. He shows up with everything I need.

Are you willing to try something new in the spiritual dimension? What's the cost...? Looking stupid? Not being good enough? Making a mistake? In your willingness, you could gain so much more than what you think you could lose. Is your comfort worth the cost of the joy from all that Christ could do?

Let God stir up new space and lead you into different spaces where you can be used in new ways. If you do something that you love, I challenge you to invite someone who might just be waiting for an invitation. Don't just talk about it...do it! Recently I was invited to go road biking; I haven't done it yet, but I'm gonna set it up! Stay tuned!!

Keep pressing on. Keep stepping out.

Don't let your past conform you into something you no longer are.

Be ready for growth and change.

I'm not sure what's next... but I am game!

NOTES

_____

_____

_____

_____

_____

Do you bring God your questions, problems, lack of understanding, and feel as if you hear nothing? Do you sometimes say, "Other people hear God but I can't? He just doesn't speak to me." Do you ever think, "I am the reason that He doesn't talk to me?" Or "something is wrong with me?" What do you do when you feel like you can't hear God? John 10:3 says:

And because the gatekeeper knows who he is, he opens the gate to let him in. And the sheep recognize the voice of the true Shepherd, for he calls his own by name and leads them out, for they belong to him.

This implies that God speaks and you will hear Him.

So, if that scripture in John is true and what you are experiencing is different, how do you stop those two from colliding in your world?

Next, most of the Bible characters are just like us. They are working people, shepherds, farmers, businessmen (and women), parents, seekers of God. We can watch them try to have a conversation with an invisible God. They paused and listened for His voice. Seeking the Voice of God, they asked God for what they needed (wisdom or military strategy) — all in a conversation with God. God remained faithful to them. He will remain faithful to you and His Word.

In 1 Samuel 30, David was in a big pickle. The struggle and what was on the line was great. Raiders had taken everything from him and his men— cattle and goods, wives and children as slaves. His own men were turning on him because of their grief. David immediately turned to the Lord to seek His advice. *8 And David inquired of the Lord, saying, "Shall I pursue this band of raiders? Will I overtake them?" God showed up and gave him specific directions. And God said to him, "Pursue, for you will certainly overtake them, and you will succeed in the rescue."*

Just like David, we have to be willing to come to God and wait for Him to answer. How long have you been willing to sit and wait for His voice? 3 seconds? 1 minute? 45 minutes? 3 hours? Would you be willing no matter how long it actually took?

When God speaks to me or you, we aren't crazy, weird, or odd. That is exactly how so many of the Bible characters lived. Sometimes what God would tell them seemed crazy to believe, yet they knew God's voice. We have to listen and know the voice of God. God speaking to you is personal. He speaks your language. The more you spend in the Word, you are hearing God and understanding how He talks.

Don't stress, God loves you very much and His desire is for you to hear Him is greater than yours. God can and will speak through people, animals, art, creation, written words, songs, however you will listen. Ask Him to speak to you in different ways, through different things. Know that He longs to speak to you.

You could journal —write out your heart to the Lord, sit and wait to hear Him. Remember you will recognize His voice. When you hear something, write whatever you hear, no matter what it is. Also, don't stress, just learn to listen and know that God is speaking to you. The more time you spend with God, the more you know Him. Where do you like to listen to God?

Listening in the car right now,

Love
Rebecca

NOTES

_____

_____

_____

_____

_____

_____

_____

_____

_____

_____

_____

_____

_____

_____

_____

_____

_____

Sitting outside writing to you today. It's nice until you find a spider climbing on you that you have to smash.... Ewwww. Hope your day has no spider smashing in it. ;)

Just so happens I was outside earlier today and heard a cry for help in the distance. At first I paused and just listened. Then I heard it again and then again. For real, someone was crying for help. I went and threw on my red hunter boots and headed into the woods in my backyard as my cousin headed down the street. As I was climbing through the woods, looking and praying we could find whoever was calling for help. I also thought of what I could possibly come across. Now, I was thinking, "Do I really want to do this?" When someone needs help, we override all those fears and scream "YES!" Inside. Someone is crying out and I hear it.

In our walks of life, we can't ignore the cries. We can't assume someone else hears the ones that have been crying out for help. We have to be like Jesus. As He walked through the streets, many yelled out to Him. Check out this..

As Jesus and his followers arrived at Jericho, a blind beggar was sitting by the roadside. When he heard the crowd approaching, he asked, "What's all this commotion about?" "It's Jesus!" they said. "Jesus the Nazarene is passing by." The blind beggar shouted, "Jesus, Son of David, have pity and show me mercy!" Those in the front of the crowd scolded him and warned him to be quiet, but the blind beggar screamed out even louder, "Jesus, Son of David, show me mercy!" Suddenly Jesus stopped and directed those nearby, "Bring the man over to me." When they brought him before Jesus, he asked the man, "What do you want me to do for you?" "Master," he said, "please, I want to see." Jesus said, "Now you will see. Receive your sight this moment, for your faith in me has given you sight and new life." Instantly he could see again. His eyes popped open, and he saw Jesus standing in front of him! He shouted loud praises to God and he followed Jesus. And when the crowd saw what happened, they too erupted with shouts of praise to God.
Luke 18:35-43

Are you walking through each day, knowing that there are people praying and asking Jesus to send someone to help them, answer them, see them? Did you know that the path you take, the job you are in, even the family you are a part of, each plays a role because God has positioned you with purpose. Just like Jesus, you can have a dynamic impact. We can't be afraid of helping people or choosing to quiet them. We can't find excuses to not step into people's lives and answer the call. Sometimes it is easy to get distracted with our pressing agenda. Kids need to be here or there. Did you get the check in the mail? When is that dentist appointment? Did you pick it up or was I supposed to? Oh no, the uniform isn't cleaned for tomorrow. Gotta get that done. SMH.

Those immediate things that demand our time during the day aren't always the most important issues that need our attention. How can we navigate our day so people, bosses, children, spouses, friends, aren't controlling our lives?

Even Jesus experienced this very problem.

Jesus chose to let His life be controlled only by the Father's plan no matter if there were other pressing issues. He understood how to see and feel what God was doing and make it of utmost importance.

Read how He handled a distraction in Luke 8:40-56. The importance of Jairus, a ruler in the synagogue was known. Jesus was directed more by what God was doing in the moment rather than Jairus. The woman with the issue of blood came through the crowds, silently crying out for healing. She reached out in faith and touched His garment. Jesus knew which was more important— Jairus or the woman— he responded with God's mercy and love. The crazy awesome thing is, the important guy Jairus and his pressing issue was not left without his answer either. God showed up on both sides of the story. It was beautiful.

For those silent cries... *you have God's ears to hear.*

Cries of the lonely... *you have God's friendship.*

Cries of the hungry... *you have God's provision.*

Cries from the weak... *you have God's strength.*

Cries of hopelessness... *you have God's encouragement.*

Cries of the dying... *you have God's resurrection power.*

Cries of the frightened... *you have God's perfect love.*

Through the Holy Spirit, you have everything that someone else needs. People are crying out silently in your life, in your neighborhood, in your church, in your job, in your family, pushing through the crowds, hoping for God's touch. He put His power in you... God is more than able to meet you and those around you.

If you are crying out for help, you can always reach out to me.

Listening and responding,

NOTES

_____

_____

_____

_____

Ever feel like you are on a roller coaster not of your own choosing? You are up and down, swirling and twisting sometimes in darkness, wondering what has to happen to get it to just stop. You scream and plead to get off, yet it starts moving at warp speed. You wish it had a big red stop button! Where is that off switch???

What if it isn't about finding an off switch?

What if it isn't about stopping the chaos, but moving through it?

Do you want it to just stop or do you really want to find yourself on the other side? We can't pause the discomfort or the struggle and just stay in it. Crazy how people have found ways to do just that.

They push the off switch in their marriages...have a fight, kick it under the carpet and never really deal with the problem.

They push the off switch in their jobs...take the most and give the least.

They push the off switch in raising their kids...as long as they come out alive, that's good enough.

In reality, the struggle creates the opportunity to make the most progress, the struggle could be an avenue for the grace and power of God to move in and through lives. What's one area where you have hit the pause button when you are supposed to be conquering? It takes grit to move through some struggles. Endurance and force is most likely necessary, too. Moving through could require dying to yourself.

The path of the righteous is level; you make level the way of righteous. Isaiah 26:7

As we seek God, He makes a level path for us and we just need to keep walking. What does your level path look like? A "path" is made for walking... not building a house and community on. We can't make our discomforts, trials, circumstances places to settle into. For real though...Have you built a house in the middle of the crazy hard places? When you come to those places, remember you can choose to continue to move past them into more of all that Christ has attained for us.

Not that I have already attained, or am already perfected; but I press on, that I may lay hold of that for which Christ Jesus has also laid hold of me. Philippians 3:12

It's not easy. Weariness, long nights, moodiness, frustrations, apathy, laziness, unbelief, doubt, and fear would love to pull you right up in the seat next to them, and have the bar come down and keep you on that up and down roller coaster as long as possible.

But, we have been given keys. Truth can replace any and all of those emotions that try to grip us and exchange them for all God is in each and every moment. One minute you can be struggling with fear... then the next minute you have His Peace. When

you are there, grab truth and let it surround you, so that you are not stopped and consumed. Move through your emotions, and keep going until you land on the Truth. Real Truth. Perhaps you need to pause and sing a verse or two of a worship song or recite the Lord's prayer. Text a friend for prayer. Take a deep breath and speak the name of Jesus until you feel His presence instead of the presence of your enemies (negative emotions). Grab the Bible and read a chapter or two until you hear God's voice above all.

Please, friend, don't feel like you are trapped on that roller coaster. You are not alone, you are with a faithful God who always has a way out. He made plans before you could even have known you would find yourself where you are. God is CONSTANT. Lean into that. He will take your crazy ups and downs, swirls and twists and make them level for you.

Counting on God to be the Leveler I need,

Becca

NOTES

_____

_____

_____

_____

_____

_____

_____

_____

_____

dear friend

Think about all those people you have been trying to reach for Jesus (planting seeds or watering): parents, long time friend, boss, childhood friend, neighbor, child, cousin, etc... What have you done to reach them? Does it feel like endless conversations have lead nowhere? Do you find yourself praying for them? Do you wonder what it's gonna take? Or do you say nothing, hoping someone else will introduce them to Jesus?

And he said to them, "The harvest is plentiful, but the laborers are few. Therefore pray earnestly to the Lord of the harvest to send out laborers into his harvest." Luke 10:2

My heart this morning is to stir you into action. First, I hope God will give you a heart for the lost. If you already do, awesome! Let it continually grow. Stir up yourself. Watch your neighbors, co-workers, or family members in a way that your heart sees their silent cries. Allow the Holy Spirit to activate your heart of compassion, love and mercy. Once your passion grows, don't sit and not let it move you. It's like having a passion to sing, but never taking the next step to actually sing.

Some Ideas of how to grow in your passion for sharing Jesus are:

+Know your Bible and learn from it how to lead someone to salvation.

+Write out your personal testimony.

+Memorize a prayer of salvation.

+Learn more and more Scriptures to stir someone's faith.

Christians have to know that it's not a format or exact words. It's not robotic. It's finding a way, with the Holy Spirit's help, for reaching each individual and leading them to Jesus, just like Jesus led people in unique ways and was so timely and specific that it shot straight into their own situation and hearts.

People need to be reached, but do you know how to introduce them to Jesus? It isn't as much about being qualified as being willing.

Preach the word; be ready in season and out of season; reprove, rebuke, and exhort, with complete patience and teaching. 2 Timothy 4:2

Since we are called to co-labor with Christ, we have to at least know how to tell someone how to be saved. One tool you can use is called the Romans Road. It can give you the ability to explain the gospel to someone through scripture. Here it is: Romans 3:23, Romans 6:23, Romans 5:8, Romans 10:9-10, Romans 10:13. It's great to memorize and have it in your "tool box".

Willingness is key. The world has created crazy patterns of busyness that causes us to focus on things that are not eternal but temporal. People are eternal; things we have and do are not. Is your impact on someone else's life going to be temporal or eternal?

Are you courageous enough to step outside of your own comfort to step into someone's discomfort for a moment? Willing to bring the answer that lives inside of you into a situation or circumstance someone is facing to lead them to Jesus? Courage comes with confidence. If we know whom we love and serve, know and understand what He did for us, we will have confidence to tell others about Him. (Ephesians 3:12)

Nothing will lead someone to Jesus better than you being real and vulnerable. Express your love for God and God's love for them. Get prepared. The lost are everywhere... waiting for us.

Willing,

NOTES

_____

_____

_____

_____

_____

_____

_____

_____

_____

_____

_____

_____

_____

_____

dear friend

How many times have you just showed up somewhere for someone? I want to challenge you today to show up for people. Don't talk about it. Just do it. Show up for people who have victories to celebrate or who are in the middle of the battle. Don't ask them if they want you to show up, just do it. If you ask, they would probably say "no", but they really wish you would.

All the weeks we were in the hospital when Romaro was ill, it was so nice when someone just showed up and we didn't have to send them a text saying, "Would you come?" Or those days when I didn't have to ask for help, but someone just showed up.

Are you thinking, "How would I even know how or when to show up???" That's part of being actively present in the lives of people around you. For example, someone randomly comes into your mind and you think, "hum…" Take that thought and ask God, "Is there a reason you brought them to my mind? Is there something needed? What can I do that I am not aware of?" The Holy Spirit will help you. You can find out and not just assume… We have to find more places where we can just show up, with no strings, or requirements. Just to love the mess out of people.

It's easy to come up with any reason why it would be better to not do something. At times, my reasons can be really lame. (Guilty). Evaluate if your second or third thoughts are more about you. For example, you think, "I'm probably not hearing anything. What would they think about me if I just showed up?" Is your hesitancy more about you or them?

So, when we show up, the situation changes from being about us, to being about other people; real people. Do you love people enough to show up? Showing up can look like a soccer game, a concert, a text, a hospital room, a waiting room, a kitchen, a car ride, a plane ride, minutes, hours, days, or even years.

In the first miracle of Jesus, John 2:1-12, Jesus shows up at a wedding. He's not there intentionally to fix any problem. He's not to be known. He's not even incredibly willing. As the problem was made known to Him, He did what we have to do: choose to do something or do nothing. He had to respond one way or another. Yet, He didn't back away. He stepped in. He showed up. You can say, "Well, Becca, it was Jesus." Yes, but you have Jesus in you. Cheers to turning water into wine! You know the answer and the miracle worker. The same power that moved then, lives inside of you. Relax. Not all places where you are asked to show up will need a miracle. Some people and places just need your hands, feet, time, ears, knowledge, etc. Think about where you're going to show up. Make it about loving people and their hearts. Invest yourself into being the answer. **Show up and love hard.** Will you show up when no one else will?

Please be willing to listen and show up. Trust Jesus with the impact on the other side.

Listening and showing up,

Love
Rebecca

NOTES

_____

_____

_____

_____

_____

_____

_____

_____

_____

_____

_____

_____

_____

_____

_____

_____

_____

_____

_____

_____

_____

_____

dear friend

Today, I'm cheering for all the single parents in the pages. I cheer you on. Keep on keeping on. For the last 5 years (as I write this) I've been a single mother. Parenting is challenging enough, but being a single parent is even moreso. I want to encourage you not to carry the weight of the full responsibility for everything. You will not see the best responses in parenting as you carry so much. Know what you are strong in, and be strong in it.

In parenting I have felt like I have to be everything CALEIGH, CADENCE, LONDON, and JUBILEIGH need a Mom and Dad, and all the in between. Since Romaro passed away, I have felt the need to fulfill both roles. In trying to be everything, I was more than tired and full of guilt for all my shortcomings. I felt guilty when I lost my temper, when I made mistakes, when I didn't want to hug at all, or when I wasn't all I wanted to be for them. My "mother's love" felt inadequate to fill them because they needed what their dad could have been for them. It was horrible and hard. That pressure, added to parenting itself, was too much.

One day a friend unknowingly gave me an important insight: the gap between what my children need and who I am is a space God created just for Himself. Call it GOD SPACE if you want. That space is designed for them to NOT look to people to meet all their needs. My children even need space for Jesus to be what they need. Friend, the thing is, there will always be a gap. Even if I was the PERFECT parent and/or Romaro were here being the best dad, it would still not be enough!

It will NEVER be enough.

All I could do would try to be something I'm not and my kids would see straight through my fake responses.

Consider bringing God into the conversation of your parenting. Talk through the how and what to do, along with all the spaces where you don't have energy, time, or ability. He can bring people to walk with us and ideas to strengthen us as we tend to our children. He can be so much more as we give Him space to do so. Along with all the other titles He qualifies Himself to do, He is the Father to the fatherless:

Father of the fatherless and protector of widows is God in his holy habitation. Psalm 68:5

When I hit a wall with my children, my first response has become, "God, what do I do? How do I do it?" Then I listen. I draw my attention away from my thoughts to whatever He is directing me, giving God space to parent from the inside of me. Thankfully, when things don't go the way I planned, He has already become the answer. He wants to be your answer. Loving and caring for my children with my strongest love language also creates space for their growth. If my strongest way of showing love doesn't fit into their specific mold, they will be pushed to grow in ways they don't know that they need. For example, I might be strong in loving them by showing them adventure, but if there is a pause or stop to that movement, it might result in growth as they consider the beauty that could be easily missed with constant activity. Growth can happen in adventure and contemplation, but it's a different growth. As a parent, I want to create spaces for divine growth. It's like giving my children breathing room. Growth is found within the protective place of love; loving them intentionally, being real, and not forcing it.

You are strong. You can do your best, but when you reach your ending point, let God fill your gap. Having a relationship with Him as a "Husband" gives you space to breathe.

I believe the best for you, friend. Really. You have an ability in you greater than you can think of or imagine, because God lives in you. Lean into Him as you parent. Don't let your mistakes and gaps fill you with guilt, when you can have God as your partner.

My gap is filling with more of Him and less of me,

Beccalove

NOTES

_____

_____

_____

_____

_____

_____

_____

_____

_____

_____

_____

_____

_____

Today is the day that Romaro passed away 4 years ago (as I wrote this)... It's been an interestingly difficult day. I felt somewhat discouraged when I look back, wondering why what I wanted to happen didn't happen. Then my thoughts spun around and I wondered what would happen in the future. I thought about all that I want to do in my future. I kept looking into the days or years ahead, wondering and wishing. Then my pondering turned to the realization that God is in the waiting. He is with us. ALWAYS.

For he has said, "I will never leave you nor forsake you." Hebrews 13:5

This is how I realized God was answering my whirling thoughts: He is not in just the big moments, or when the prophetic word is released, but in each and every moment. Today. Right where your feet are placed. Go ahead, look down. God is there, in that place. God will do what He has promised you. What's He doing in this moment of your life? Can amazing things happen today? Are you looking for them? Go ahead and take hold of what God is doing.

If you didn't have tomorrow, would you be satisfied with what you did today? Not yesterday or the past, but today. **Live today.** Don't live for the hype of a trip, or the next big thing, but be fully present in your today. When I was a child, I lived for the high moments, the big days, and wished many days would pass so quickly so I could get to what I thought was a BIG deal. In reality, I wasted days. I wasted opportunities. I wasted time. As I concentrated on the destination, the journey seemed pointless.

The world has made certain dates to be highlighted, so we wait and watch the calendar. Our whole week sometimes can be just waiting for the weekend. Our best days are the ones that we look forward to, like a holiday or vacation. This waiting for the big day as we skip the journey to get to the holiday is a pattern of the world system. Those hyped or big moments come and go, but each day holds the possibility for an experience that could lead us to experience more of God. The journey is where we find God.

What if you were given moment's in your journey where you could make an eternal difference in someone's life? Each day you could ask the Lord for opportunities to reach the lost. If our focus is held captive to the next big thing, or day, you won't see the middle and what could be. For instance, what if one sentence said to someone caused increased momentum in their gifts and led them to new beginnings? What if your kindness caused someone to come to Jesus, causing an eternal impact?

As our example, as Jesus journeyed from one place to the next, He saw people, stepped into their world, and shifted everything. He didn't wait for the big days such as the Passover, or the big crowd. He was present for each person— those who cried out, the persistent ones with pain or questions. He fully embraced the fullness of each day... listening, obeying, and being fully present. God wants to live in us like that.

Jesus wants each day for you to make an eternal impact on the earth. He loves the big days you look forward to, but He wants to be Lord over our every day. Fully alive, present... in our thoughts and our actions. The only way you can do this is by seeing God in the middle, seeing God in the waiting.

Part of my story of growth in this is all the days spent in a hospital wishing for the big day/moment when Romaro would be healed. I prayed and contended for the miracle, yet I hated where we were. At the beginning, I hated every second that we sat waiting... until I realized that I could continue to believe and find God in the waiting. I chose to enjoy and take our waiting as an opportunity to be with Romaro, as well as seeing what God could do through us in the hospital.

When the Bible talks about Paul being in prison, it shows us that if he wouldn't have been in prison, he wouldn't have had the opportunity to reach certain people for the gospel. Maybe whatever you are in the middle of, is an opportunity for God to position you in the right place so you can make an eternal impact! If our lives are truly surrendered to the Lord, and our YES is 100%, then wherever we are, whatever it looks like, we can be fully present, willing and fully knowing God has positioned us there purposefully. In the waiting, in the small moments, in the big moments, or in the "middle", He positions us for purpose. Please, don't run away from uncomfortable moments; know and trust they could become the places you have the greatest impact. But in the middle, you have to trust and look for God. He is there, friend. Ask Him to show you just where He is and what He is interested in doing in and through you.

Looking for God in the middle,

NOTES

_____

_____

_____

_____

_____

_____

_____

dear friend

DAY THIRTY EIGHT

__ / __ / __

So today, I find myself watching my littles run at the park, thinking of you and where today has found you. Pausing to pray an unexpected blessing for you today. Asking God to speak specifically to you at this moment. Will you pause, look around and just wait?

God is watching you like I am my children. He is watching and enjoying who you are. He loves you, friend. If you are lonely today, He is with you. If you can only see your imperfections, which you are hoping to correct before He sees them, you are not hidden. You are known by Him. He knows those thoughts which seem to be hidden, lost in translation, winding down a trail no one seems to know. He hears those thoughts, too. There are no secrets within His creation. He is fully aware of everything. If you wonder who even cares, He cares. The best part is, He longs to be with you.

Behold, I'm standing at the door, knocking. If your heart is open to hear my voice and you open the door within, I will come in to you and feast with you, and you will feast with me.
Revelation 3:20

He longs for you. He is actually jealous of all the other things that steal your attention. He doesn't want just the pieces of your heart, but the whole of you. It is easy sometimes to let our conversations with God become the same run-on requests. Letting your time with God always stay on the surface, never any deeper. It's like a door is between you and Him. You talk through the door and don't choose to open it for Him, for fear of what could happen or what He would see. He knocks, waiting for you to allow Him in for a conversation that is heart to heart. Will you allow Him in? Do you want to go deeper?

Are you always crying, complaining to Him and never really conversing? Have you been stuck on the "same ole, same ole" for the past five years? Have you felt, as you say "amen," that you have no idea what you even said, but expecting Him to answer?

God wants to draw you into table conversations.

(Did you just ask yourself, "What is a table conversation???") It's the type of conversation when you aren't just coming to him to cry about what's wrong, what you need, what you want fixed. It's more of a conversation where you share and then He shares. You express your heart and then He expresses His. It's a place of sharing, not one-sidedness. Just so happens,He desires to come in and sit with you, having table conversations that get deep. Re-read Revelation 3:20 above. The time to talk is as long as you stay. He is interested in listening to all your excitement, thoughts, and desires, and letting you in all that He has for you.

Call to me and I will answer you, and will tell you great and hidden things
that you have not known. Jeremiah 33:3

Now, THAT is a conversation! We have to create space for that. I keep telling one of my friends, "I'm here to listen, if you want to talk, the space is open." With God the space is always open, talk to Him about those secret things, the hard things, the best things, that one thing you have never talked to God about before. If it works better to write out your prayers, write them out. After you write, write His response. Seriously.

It might be breaking out of our normal conversations to talk about something 'out of the box' then listen for His response. Don't think you are in a fast food line with God. "I want.... Here's my money," and you are out. Sit with God. How long are you willing to sit and wait?

Think about going to a restaurant— how long have you waited to be seated??? Longest I have waited was two hours! I know, just for food. EWWW! I was willing to wait that long for something that had no real value. I don't know the last time I sat and talked to God for over two hours...dang.

How long are you willing to wait at the table to hear the Lord speak to you? For the God of the universe, Creator of time, to speak to you about eternal things, about what's going on, or the things that will satisfy the longing of your soul. Don't wonder if the wait is worth it. It is always worth it and He will always show up! ALWAYS.

If you are waiting, know I'm waiting, too!

NOTES

_____

_____

_____

_____

_____

_____

_____

_____

dear friend

If someone gave you a hundred bucks this morning and told you to go have fun, what would you choose to do? Would you go shopping? Go on an adventure? Give it away? Do 10 random acts of kindness? Pay a bill? Do nothing, because you would be afraid to make the wrong decision? Maybe you are thinking, "$100 bucks? I can't do much with that."

So, what if someone gave you a thousand dollars? What would you do then? Would you split it between doing something for you and something for someone else? Would you totally pay off a debt? Would you give it all away?

Just for the sake of conversation, pick something, please.

What is your decision for the 100 bucks?

What is your decision for the 1000 buckaroos?

Those adventures, spaces of giving, and so much more are available for us each and every day. In our faith walk, we are called to see what we will do with what we have. In John 6:1-15, the disciples had fish and the loaves. Jesus called out His disciples asking, "What are you gonna do about all these hungry people?" By faith we are called out to live. What do you have? A jar of coins? An extra $10?

Have you asked God, "What can you do with my little?"

You have so little compared to Him, even if you are a millionaire/billionaire. Yet you possess the greatest resource: a willing heart. How willing is your heart? Measure it. Really measure it.

If God asked you to go to Africa, would you get packing? Apply for your passport?

If God asked you to adopt a child, would you get a bedroom ready? Fill out the paperwork?

If God asked you to sponsor a child with Compassion International, would you call and do it? How long would it take?

If God asked you to start singing at church, would you fill out the volunteer application?

If God asked you to start a Bible study, would you invite someone over? Would you begin reading and studying your Bible? The list could go on and on...

And I heard the voice of the Lord saying, "Whom shall I send, and who will go for us?" Then I said, "Here I am! Send me." Isaiah 6:8

Can you only do those kinds of things based on the "it just so happens I was given money?" God has asked, "May I use your hands? May I use your feet?" If we are always looking only at what we have, we will always do whatever we can do, and never lean into all He has. When we step into places where we don't have what it takes, and we don't have enough, we step across the line of faith from "us" into "God and us," which is where impossibility lives. Will you decide to have your "Yes" be "Yes," no matter what? Are you willing to say, "God whatever, whenever, I'm game?" Being willing to listen and follow God is when and where you live your faith out loud. Did I just hear you say, "Bec, yeah, I get what you are saying...but I live in reality." But friend, God is asking His righteous ones to live by faith:

But my righteous one shall live by faith, and if he shrinks back, my soul has no pleasure in him. Hebrews 10:38

Faith is an adventure; it's hearing God and obeying Him regardless of what makes sense. It's trusting God because you know He has the resources and He comes through. If He has done it for others, He will do it for you.

I challenge you to cross the line. Jump actually. Don't hesitate. He is on the other side. It's not a moment of risk but the beginning of a life of living. Friend, there isn't time to waste. Be ready to jump quickly and obey the very moment God speaks. Have your YES card permanently ready at all times. ALWAYS.

The line is farther than ever, and my "Yes!" is louder than fear,

Rebeca Yone

NOTES

_____

_____

_____

_____

_____

How are you? Was your answer, "ok"? Did you think, "I'm fine"? What was your next statement? If there is something you need to tell someone, I'm here, message me. I'm actually willing to listen. If it is heartbreak or struggle, something joyous or sad, if it is a small victory or a big defeat or if there is something you just wish you could tell someone, pop me a message.

Today, I'm going to be real and confess I am having a day full of a messy heart. My car just broke and I have been looking for a car. It went from wanting to being pushed into needing a car. I feel like here is the deep end, do I trust what God has told me? I believe God has a car for my family, but it is currently not in my vision yet. So by faith, I am believing. Let's say it's one of those days when my faith is put to the test. Along with "Am I living what I am saying?" How close do those two things line up? For example, I say I trust God. Right? We all confess [or profess], shout and sing, "I trust in you." But when the day comes that God says, "Trust me, Becca" in a situation that looks overly complicated, possibly impossible and I have no resources, will I choose to trust God or do I grab my heart and run so I can protect it? Man, my heart has been feeling like that— protect it from the "what if's", all the unknowns, the possibilities of it being hurt or disappointed.

Recently, in a conversation with a friend, I shared the really raw stuff with her. **I realized how much of what I *felt* wasn't what I wanted to *believe*.** The feelings were contrary to what I know is true. I cried, giving God space to show me what He really has for me and my children. I made a decision to lean into God instead of giving into my feelings. That decision felt good.

Open up your heart often to see what's happening in there. Don't shield your heart with your words and/or your thoughts. Be willing to expose those places and let God inside.

Keep creating in me a clean heart. Fill me with pure thoughts and holy desires, ready to please you. Psalm 51:10

So when was the last time you encouraged a friend to talk and you really listened? When you choose to go deeper than the surface, something beautiful can happen. You don't have to know all the answers. You don't even have to know what to say.

Iron sharpens iron, and one man sharpens another. Proverbs 27:17

Once a friend didn't know what to say after I shared something deep, so she looked at me and said, "Now, just imagine me telling you exactly what you need to hear." That comment was so true and clear, so refreshing that we laughed and laughed. I didn't need perfect advice, only a friend willing to listen and pray. Someone willing to be real and say, "I'm not sure what to say, but I am here."

Now, how about the last time you opened space for your children to share what is happening in their world? Have you asked them about their hearts lately? What's one of their biggest struggles? Be willing to invest in friends and family by simply listening. Jesus would.

I challenge you to choose four friends and check in on them this week. After they share with you, pray with them in person, even if it shocks them. If you accept the challenge, believe when you pray, and ask the Father for big and bold things on their behalf. Don't hesitate to ask God to use you to minister to them. We are called to pray for one another.

Embrace the power of salvation's full deliverance, like a helmet to protect your thoughts from lies. And take the mighty razor-sharp Spirit-sword of the spoken word of God. Pray passionately in the Spirit, as you constantly intercede with every form of prayer at all times. Pray the blessings of God upon all his believers. Ephesians 6:17-18

If you don't know what to say, use what my friend told me, and then laugh a little. Lol!! Know that God is faithful to speak through you and use you if you are willing to push beyond what is comfortable. Remember that your comfort isn't what is the most important, our call to love people as Jesus loves is:

For when you demonstrate the same love I have for you by loving one another, everyone will know that you're my true followers. John 13:35

What if at the other side of your willingness is the miracle the person sitting next to you has been crying out for? Wouldn't that be amazing!!! What if it is a "just so happens" moment? It just so happens they were wanting more and you were the more that they were asking God for. Don't worry about planning the when, what and how, only offer the willingness of your heart and your yes.

Show up. Listen. Love. It's simple....it just requires Jesus.

Trusting God for the words,

Love
Rebecca

PS. I got a car and God did answer. It was awesome too!!!

NOTES

_____

_____

_____

Hi, I hope you are doing well. I am currently sitting and writing to you in a coffee shop while my kids are drawing beside me. Been just thinking and praying for you today. Life is an adventure, so what do you want out of today? Take the opportunity to live it out. Are you gonna go after it? May God cause you to hope beyond measure.

Faith is a lifestyle. He calls us to live by faith.

He calls us into deep places where impossible things live.

When you read the last sentence, did you want to run towards faith places or run from them? Do you live with your faith activated?

I didn't realize how hard writing would be in the midst of the "Mom," "Mom" (on repeat 42 times daily, multiply by 4 children) lol. There are always distractions when we do life; life just happens around us. Your opportunities can be rich, but full of distractions. Understand that there are purposes in some of the obstacles. You may be learning to multitask, to sharpen your ability to focus, to discern between the important and the trivial. At those times when we keep going, and refuse to give up, we learn to persevere. But above all, don't let distractions hinder God's purpose for you.

What are your opportunities? What is God asking you to do?_____
[Take some time to pray about it and then fill in the blank.]

It has been said, "If it is important to you, you will make time, and if distractions come you will distract them with your willingness to keep going." Each day has opportunities… look for them. We can so easily get in the mode of "it just so happens"… and yet, in the middle of "happens," God cultivates opportunities for us to be a servant of God, living out the fullness of the potential He created in us. We have to live with our eyes wide open, watching to see how God will move, looking for the opportunities He puts in front of us. Life is not just "whatever happens, happens," but God's plan being worked out.

We are his workmanship, created in Christ Jesus for good works, which God prepared beforehand, that we should walk in them. Ephesians 2:10

Today, God has personally crafted opportunities for you to walk into and live out. These are not merely coincidences, but God-personalized assignments for you to do. Are you walking in those things? Are you living like God created space for you to do something that no one else could? Do you live with this mandate in your spirit?

So then, as we have opportunity, let us do good to everyone, and especially to those who are of the household of faith. Galatians 6:10

What good are you going to do in the world? Who will your good be directed towards today? How often are you willing to do good? Once a month? Once a year? Once a week? Where are you to release it?

When Jesus was walking around on the earth He was always willing to do the good prepared for him to do.

He did good to people in want as much as in need. (Matthew 14:13-21)

He did good for His buddies. (John 21:1-14)

He did good for those who walked by. (Luke 19:1-10)

He walked all day long with people in mind, not tasks.

So, how do I affect people?

Show them His love, His grace, and His power to be good. Represent Jesus to those that are on the earth.

Use every opportunity, not just the perfect ones.

Let God work in us to accomplish His will on the earth.

Let our lives be more His and less ours.

Let our time be marked by Him and perfect in His timing.

Give of yourself, and give Big.

The saying is trustworthy, and I want you to insist on these things, so that those who have believed in God may be careful to devote themselves to good works. These things are excellent and profitable for you. Titus 3:8

Letting His plan become mine,

When was the last time you just showed up for God? Showed up and let God have a whole hour of your day? Do you ever think, "I will just show up and see what God can do through me?" Are you waiting for the perfect timing? Perfect circumstances?

I was just texting my friend, and it went like this:

ME: I wish I were better at multitasking ...(not one of my gifts)

HER: Keep writing.

ME: I am. My kids can make it so difficult.

ME: Seriously.

HER: Yeah, sorry...

ME: It's ok... Learning to work through it.

ME: And have patience.

ME: And courage to not wait for the perfect moments!

ME: That's me... wanting life to be easy, lol

Is that the atmosphere I demand—perfect? We can do that...wait for the perfect, easiest moments before acting on what God has said to us. We can wait for things to align, yet God calls us to move forward in faith, even when we don't feel ready. He calls us to show up, and let Him show up with whatever we need. Not depending on what we are, but relying on who He is.

Putting faith in action requires a learning curve.

We need to work on showing up in our marriages, in our parenting, in kingdom work, in our communities, in our relationships, in whatever He is asking, without questions; showing up fully, and saying YES. Would God have a full "yes" from you if He asked you to go to Uganda? What if He asked you to homeschool your children? Would you show up, say yes, no questions? What about dating your wife once a week? Serving in the nursery? Give above your comfort level? Praying for someone walking by?

How much do we have to know before we say yes? How comfortable do we have to be to obey what God is saying? God doesn't ask us to do something and then not show up for us. He said He would never leave us nor forsake us.

So be strong and courageous! Do not be afraid and do not panic before them. For the Lord your God will personally go ahead of you. He will neither fail you nor abandon you.
Deuteronomy. 31:6

What if you didn't show up when God asked? What miracles would you miss in order to stay comfortable? What opportunities would you give up, because you didn't know everything? What relationships would suffer, because you said No instead of Yes?

We can't let the unknown keep us from doing because God knows the unknown for us. Each day we need to wake up with a "Yes, God." Try it for a week. We can't let distractions keep us from doing; we have to keep our focus on God. We can't let our natural ability or resources hold us back, when He is our very source.

SO many times, I have been distracted by this or that as I sit to write. All kinds of reasons why I can't, and all the uncertainties of how or even what to write, can consume me. Yet faith calls to me above all that, and I say Yes to God. I show with my pen and watch Him show up with all the rest.

What does God want to bring through you on the earth that you haven't done yet? Was your second thought a reason why you couldn't do it?

Let's live a life that is fully surrendered, fully committed, fully willing. Let's give God a full YES. No excuses. Take hold of His plan, and by faith, work it. Take at least one step this week. You could read the story of Abraham in Genesis 12. He had the Biggest "YES"es I know:

Yes, I will move...even though you are not telling me where I'm going.

Yes, I will believe your promise...even though I don't have any children.

Yes, I will keep being intimate with my wife...even though my body is dead.

Yes, now that I have a son...I will go and sacrifice him.

Yes, I will have faith to believe you.

Yes, I will hold nothing back from you.

Yes, whatever you want, Lord.

Yes, all of me is all yours.

Say Yes! I am,

Beccalove

NOTES

_____

_____

_____

_____

What's one of your biggest fears??

It's too easy to come to a place where fears become commonplace. When we easily say, "I am afraid of...." Have you made those fears part of who you are? If so, then you likely don't feel any pressure or need to address or change them. We just let them ride in our pocket and travel with us. But sometimes they really show their ugly faces. Fears can easily change our course, our destination. Fears can easily unmotivate us to try things. Fears can keep us moving in a direction that goes nowhere. Often we become a slave to the fear.

Fear of what people might think.

Fear of what people might say, and how they might react.

Fear of the unknown.

Fear of messing everything up.

Fear of _____ (fill in the blank).

Basically fear affects each of us to a degree...some more than others. Like if you are afraid of elevators and you need to get to the 20th floor, the effect on your body after 20 flights of stairs might be significant. Some fears we keep hidden; we try not to let them surface because we don't really want to deal with them. If you have any fear, let God's Word work:

Fear not, little flock, for it is your Father's good pleasure to give you the kingdom.
Luke 12:32

Over 365 times in the Bible, God tells us to not fear. So don't! Simple huh? Maybe, we need to convince ourselves that it really is that simple and just stop fearing. Don't over think. Don't hesitate. Free yourself from the grip of fear, already lost to the God that lives in you.

No, in all these things we are more than conquerors through him who loved us.
Romans 8:37

Friend, really I want to ask you if your fears are holding someone else back. Because you are afraid, do you hold your husband/wife back? Your children back? Your friends? Seriously, think about it. Do a heart check.

Do you keep people closest to you in a cage of sorts...where they can't fully live because you are afraid of what could or could not happen to them? Don't trap people in your fears. For instance, if you are afraid of flying, will your children never go anywhere that is beyond driving? Your fear of what bad may happen will keep them grounded. Think of all the places they will never see or experience.

When we hold people back, what are we truly holding them from?

What could you release your husband/wife into that would enable them to flourish in places you never dreamt? Are your children living with potential locked inside them? If only you would let them fly! Or do you hold them back?

Fear can actually replace faith unless you are willing to trust God enough to release those you love. Search your heart; ask yourself, "Do I hold someone back because of my own fears?" If you find a yes, deal with it head on. Release the person. Pour love and faith into the situation instead of pulling away. Let God love the mess out of you and live without boundaries of fear.

There is no fear in love, but perfect love casts out fear. For fear has to do with punishment, and whoever fears has not been perfected in love.
1 John 4:18

Fearless in life,

NOTES

_____

_____

_____

_____

_____

_____

_____

_____

_____

_____

Do you drive on the dot of the speed limit, or five over, maybe ten over...?

Limits are everywhere... speed limits, limits on time, limits on abilities, limits on resources. Limits on this and that. We live with so many limits. Do your limits box you in? When and where do you break the limits? Limits can have wisdom (like speed limits), yet they can also become a barrier. We learn limits from the time we are children. Did your mom or dad ever say to you, "You can't, because you are not old enough..." "You can't do that because you are not tall enough..." "You can't because you aren't smart enough." "You can't because... " We keep learning limits as we grow older. Have you adapted what you can or can't do based on limits? Skill? Talents?

Jesus looked at them and said, "With man it is impossible, but not with God. For all things are possible with God." Mark 10:27

God has no limits. NONE.

Seriously, there are none. Reread that verse. Now is the time to exchange your limits for God's limitlessness. In your own flesh, you are limited, but with the power of the Holy Spirit you have no limits. Let's learn to step out of our normal and live in the fullness God has called us to.

Men and women have prayed and the earth was changed. Men, women, and children believed and changed the world. Have you put limits on your faith? Read Hebrews 11. This list called "The Hall of Faith" goes on & on about people who believed against the odds, against what limited man. Do you think there is a limit on how much you can have? Have you found a limit on what God can give? Do you think limits are based on one person to the next? Natural things cause us to think or believe that with God we can only have so much. But the truth is, God told us to believe in Him who takes off all the limits.

For NOTHING will be impossible with God. Luke 1:37

Seriously, there is freedom because He actually invited you into a place that has no boundaries, or limits. Let nothing, not even yourself, hold you back.

So how do you step into a life that is limitless?

Number 1: Take a step into the unlimited and see where you land. Hebrews 10:38

Number 2: Don't hesitate. If your faith finds a path, press in. Hebrews 10:23

Number 3: Remember the greatness of the God you serve. He created everything you see and feel. He has the power to do anything and everything. Hebrews 12:2

Number 4: Believe and know your faith in Him pleases God. Hebrews 11:6

Let's take off the limits and see what's possible. (I just feel such an excitement in that statement!)

Becca

NOTES

_____

_____

_____

_____

_____

_____

_____

_____

_____

_____

_____

_____

_____

_____

_____

Did you eat ice cream today?? I love ice cream!! Life is full of good things (like ice cream) and grace. But sometimes we come to thresholds in our life...a door pops open to opportunities laden with unknowns. What makes you jump through the door of that opportunity?

This past week I went cliff jumping. By the way, I am not in the habit of flinging myself off of cliffs. I was super excited. But when I got on the top of the rock, instead of just jumping straight out and down, I thought way too much about it. I stood there for a long time!! (But who's counting??) I was not ready.

I didn't want to do it, but this kind of opportunity only comes every once in a great while (mainly because I don't live where cliffs are common). Standing on the top, looking down, I thought, "Will I ever again be on a rock this high and able to jump off of it?" I wanted to jump, but my mind was talking way too much and too loudly, convincing me that all my fears were reality. All the unknowns, all the fears rose from the waters below me, and all the things that could happen were screaming louder than the excitement and thrill of doing something crazy adventurous. I stood at an impasse. I walked close to the edge then backed up, over and over again. I talked to myself. I talked to God. I was afraid. That gap between excitement and fear grew bigger and bigger the longer I stood there.

So I did the only sensible thing. I jumped. I felt the air pass by me, stomach full of butterflies as I fell through the air before I plummeted into the deep water. It was exciting and empowering. My first thought was, "I have to do that again!" Crazy huh? 14 feet of crazy awesome! I climbed back up to those very same rocks. I got to the edge of the same cliff...only to be met by all the same feelings and all the same voices. I stood in the same place and didn't want to do it again, yet, I did want to do it! I thought, "I've already done this. It should be easy this time."

Really, why wasn't it? It was just as hard the second time.

That day, I ended up jumping off that cliff four times. Each time, you guessed it, I felt the same way... the same fears and the same excitement.

Living and walking by faith is similar to jumping off a cliff. Each time we have to take the first step. Each time we face the choice between fear and the execution, but we can trust God. We get to know trust in places where we have some sort of hesitation. What will happen if I step out? Will God step in?

I remember the men and women in the Bible we read about in the faith chapter. Each time they chose to push past their fears and step out in obedience to God, not fully knowing what God would do, but trusting in Him, it was labeled faith.

Trust is defined as: "firm belief in the reliability, truth, ability, or strength of someone or something" (Google.com)

Trust that God is who He says He is.

Trust in His Name.

Trust in who He had been before.

God said to Moses, "I AM WHO I AM." And he said, "Say this to the people of Israel: 'I AM has sent me to you." Exodus 3:14

At those thresholds that carry the potential to our life or someone else's life, what will we choose to do? Do we stand so long that we never move one way or another because we are comfortable standing in the door? How long will we stand there? God is waiting with you, asking you to step out, to live a life of faith, not to back out or shy away just because we can't figure out the outcome.

Why do we think we have to know everything?? Seriously, doesn't that cause us to not actually have to use our faith? Truth is, you do know the One who knows the details. The unknowns and the stepping forward when it's not all perfectly clear, builds faith. If I told you each time you stepped out in faith, it would get easier, I would be lying. One step of faith doesn't always make the next step easier. But God is constant, faithful and He is in the future waiting for us to arrive by faith.

I am the Alpha and the Omega, the first and the last, the beginning and the end. Revelation 22:13

He knows the beginning and the end, and we don't. Therefore, the way He moves and how He orchestrates things won't necessarily look like what we imagine. But I know His plan will far exceed what we could ever do. When you step out, trust that God is with you, even if it's unconventional, an unmarked path, unknown territory, an illogical request. The difference between His thoughts and ours requires faith and trust. So, when you are standing on the ground between jumping off the cliff and climbing back down, let your faith explode and push back all those things that keep trying to pull you back. Jump and keep jumping.

Faith is yours to live out.

Live it out loud.

Live it fearless.

Live it brave.

I tell myself to live like that. Do by faith whatever God asks of you. Do it when afraid, if you have to. Do whatever it is **with God.**

For all you cliff jumpers... jump with me,

Hi! I went and visited the ARK Encounter in Kentucky. It was pretty sweet and well worth the trip. It stirred up so many things I never really thought about when, as a child, I was told about Noah. Things like all the sounds the ship would have carried with it, all the feelings, the crazy darkness, and all the questions of, "What do we do now?" Going there released my imagination to wonder what Noah and his family endured. I'm sure each visitor to the Ark will take away something different because God will meet each individually. The boat had a lot of spaces for each person to encounter Him.

As we walked through the ark, we came to the section that showed how gross sin in the world was; how horrible it made God feel, how much He hated it, how it crept in and grew in the heart of man. Each person's sin was different; each was detestable to God. The Bible tells us our heart is evil continually to the point God regretted He had made man (Genesis 6:5-8). Except for Noah...

My heart sank as I was confronted with displays of the ancient world's wickedness. The reality hit me—our world is so much like theirs. So much sin. So much tolerance of sin. So much! Sin is the one thing that separates us from God. He created us to be close to Him each and every day, yet sin separates us from our Father. A sin is not little or big, all sin is sin. Have you been living in sin long enough to be comfortable with it? For real? Do we need to repent of the sin of lying? Hate? Lust? Greed? Unbelief?

> *For by grace you have been saved through faith. And this is not your own doing; it is the gift of God. Ephesians 2:8*

To be covered by God's grace and promise is greater than I can understand.

Much later in history, after Noah had been saved by God's grace, the earth was again full of the wickedness of a broken covenant. This time, God sent His son Jesus, to be born as one of us, live perfectly, and die instead of us. He became sin, so we wouldn't have to die in our sins. He died so we could live free.

> *For freedom Christ has set us free; stand firm therefore, and do not submit again to a yoke of slavery. Galatians 5:1*

God wants us to deal with our sin by covering it with His blood. I was there standing in the middle of that HUGE ark, remembering only 8 people with all the animals were on it to be saved. Was God hopeful more people would change their minds and choose Him? During the hundred years it took to build that ark, was God extending grace, hoping that maybe more would join Noah and his family?

Our world today is full of wickedness. You see it at every turn, right? Just watch at your job. Watch the news. Watch your own heart. Yet God delays His return in judgement because He wants more of the heart of men to turn. There is still more room at the cross.

The LORD is not slow to fulfill his promise as some count slowness, but is patient toward you, not wishing that any should perish, but that all should reach repentance. 2 Peter 3:9

He really loves us. He desires us to turn from the sin that keeps us from Him and run into His arms of grace. He longs for each and every person on the earth to come to Him. Hiding sin from God is not an option because each of us is fully known by Him.

Noah was a righteous man, blameless in his generations. He walked with God. Genesis 6:9

If we want God to be able to trust us to help our generation, we are to be righteous and blameless like Noah. We have to walk with God. I'm calling out your sin, just as I am talking to myself. If you are sinning...Stop it! If you are struggling and can't find a way out, get some people in your corner to help you stay on track.

Noah's sons and wives helped him build. They were a team; they did it together, not alone. Don't live alone in your sin. Don't live thinking no one understands. ALL have sinned. We are ALL sinners, but because of Jesus, we can live in victory over our sin. Trust in God's plan of redemption and freedom. The cost of what God asked of Noah was huge.

"Hey, Noah, build an ark! I know it has never rained, but build a boat. It just so happens it's only going to take you 100 years to actually finish it. Oh, and day in and day out, people will mock you. You will get tired of doing the same thing. You will come to hate the smell of pitch by the time you finish. You will leave behind all the people who won't join you. You will sweat in pain from carrying all that wood. You will struggle and grow weary. I also want you to get all the food on board for you, your family, and the animals you'll be living with for a year or so. You don't have to find the animals, I will send them to you. I need you, Noah, to keep those animals alive."

The cost is evident: whether it is the cost of sin, which leads to death, or the cost of living for God, which leads to life. The cost is real. Which will you choose?

Please friend, don't choose sin. Sin isn't worth it. Stay focused on what God is doing in your life. What He has spoken. Stay close to Him. Be like Noah and walk with God in righteousness and blamelessness.

You are not walking alone,

Beccalove

NOTES

_____

_____

_____

dear friend

If the enemy could completely take you out, he would.

Can we talk about the undeniable fact the devil wants to kill you?

> *He wants to use your own thoughts, your own words, your own ideas to destroy you. He comes to only steal, KILL and destroy. John 10:10*

His mission is no secret. Satan's mission is death. Death to your dreams, to your abilities, to your flesh. He comes against each and every single person, so welcome to the club. He may use different tactics, different resources, different voices, but it's the same mission. Reread John 10:10 again.

It's important for us to be aware of the ways the enemy wants to take us out, but we must understand the truth of God's mission which is the exact opposite—God wants for us to have life and life more abundantly. Look at the rest of the verse:

> *The thief comes only to steal and kill and destroy.*
> *But I came that they may have life and have it abundantly. John 10:10*

Suicide happens around us, everyday.

When you blow it, when you are lonely, when you are heartbroken, overwhelmed, fearful, struggling...do thoughts of death come? Do you pause and fight your thoughts?

> *We destroy arguments and every lofty opinion raised against the knowledge of God, and take every thought captive to obey Christ. 2 Corinthians 10:5*

Captive is a term of action. Be active in your thoughts. Don't struggle alone; tell someone. Don't expect your best friends to be mind readers. Don't think your parents will just know how you are feeling. Please talk or confide in someone. At least ask them to pray for you. Start somewhere, please. The devil doesn't fight fair. So fight back with an army.

Thoughts come and go, but if a person decides to house them and give them room, they are not taken "captive"; instead they become an unwelcome permanent resident. Learn to evict the thoughts that want to kill you. I honestly don't believe anyone is permanently exempt from having thoughts that are death. Perhaps currently you aren't struggling, but you don't know the thoughts of those around you. There is the possibility someone is dealing with packaging their thoughts, trekking through them, and/or trying not to drown in them.

> *For who knows a person's thoughts except the spirit of that person, which is in him? So also no one comprehends the thoughts of God except the Spirit of God. Now we have received not the spirit of the world, but the Spirit who is from God, that we might understand the things freely given us by God. 1 Corinthians 2:11-12*

For who has understood the mind of the Lord so as to instruct him?
But we have the mind of Christ. 1 Corinthians 2:16

God has given you the mind of Christ. He has His home there, too; not just in the cozy place in your heart. He lives in all of you, including your mind.

Submit yourselves to God. Resist the devil, and he will flee from you. James 4:7

Life is a gift you never get back. A priceless gift! Look around at your life. Find things that speak of the abundant life God has given you. Stir your heart with thanksgiving.
1 Thessalonians 5:18

If you aren't dealing with thoughts that are suicidal, thank God, and give grace to everyone you interact with because you don't know what they are thinking or walking through.

Let your speech at all times be gracious and pleasant, seasoned with salt, so that you will know how to answer each one. Colossians 4:6

Life is worth living. Life always changes and always can get better, don't give up.

You can always reach out.

Message me,

NOTES

_____

_____

_____

_____

_____

_____

_____

_____

Are you going through your daily grind, feeling like you want so much more? Do you feel you are wasting time, your God-given talents and purpose? Do you want to make more impact and accomplish more, but not sure how?

Does God have your attention now?

Consider your job—are you there only for the money? Are you there just to clock in and clock out? If that's your only motive, let's take another look through God's eyes (with His help). What if your job is your mission field? What if God chose you as His instrument to love your coworkers, to introduce the lost to their savior and encourage others to come into the full knowledge of God? What would you do or say if the opportunity opened up before you to tell someone about what Jesus has done for you?

How about being zealous about the second greatest commandment—love people:

And a second is like it: You shall love your neighbor as yourself. Matthew 22:39

If you ask and open yourself to Him, He will reveal to you the places that you could step into that would feed your hunger for using your talents. You are a Kingdom person and should live with a Kingdom mindset.

Open up to a new view, God's view, and add passion, intensity, fervency to whatever you do.

Someone is waiting for you to step into their world and bring spirited excitement that refreshes them. When are you going to allow and even encourage yourself to get passionate about something God is passionate about? Are you thinking, "I want to have God's passion, Becca, but I don't know what it is." Pause right now and pray for God to give you a creative idea that might ignite your spirit and soul—that's passion. I am praying with you and for you, to catch His vision.

Seek first the KINGDOM of God and his righteousness,
and all the things will be added to you. Matthew 6:33

As you seek God's kingdom, don't get bogged down with the mundane. Don't hesitate to step into the unknown when God's energy comes alive in you. Always seek first His Kingdom. Look clearly and deeply at what God is doing and has been doing in your life.

Where has God been in these areas of your life: your relationships with God and man, your work, your leisure, your future? God fits into places we tend to ignore Him. He actually wants to be the most important part of all those areas in your life to make them better than you ever imagined. Add some wood to the fire of passion. Keep it alive. We don't need a bunch of duds in our Christian community; we need people who are set on fire by the CONSUMING FIRE!

For our God is a consuming fire. Hebrews 12:29

Will you stir up God's passion lying dormant and waiting?

Stirring it up for the Kingdom,

Love
Rebecca

NOTES

_____

_____

_____

_____

_____

_____

_____

_____

_____

_____

_____

_____

_____

_____

_____

_____

_____

Hi from Chicago!! So many people here. I wonder how many of them are worrying. Worrying about someone they love, a bill, health problems, where they will sleep. Walking and watching, I wondered what you are worried about...things we wish could feel free enough to share with someone. I am sharing with you my failure and lesson of that day.

On my way to the smoothie shop to meet with a friend, I walked past a man asking for help; into the smoothie shop I went, thinking I would get him a smoothie, too. After deciding which flavors my friend and I would get, we waited in line, chatting, and I totally forgot all about everything but my treat. I ordered and walked away to wait for my drink. My friend lingered, talking to the seller, and I wondered what was taking her so long. She joined me with a cup in each hand— one for the man outside that I had so quickly forgotten. It was disheartening and convicting that I had forgotten so fast. I knew Hebrews 13:16 says:

> Do not **neglect** to do good and to **share** what you have for such sacrifices are pleasing to God.

Neglect: *"to pay no attention to too little attention to; disregard or slight".* I neglected to pay attention to doing good for that man outside the smoothie shop. I initially was willing to share, but neglected to follow through, consumed more about my own desires. Sharing is so elementary; we teach toddlers to do so. The writer of Hebrews tells us boldly: SHARE. To please God, we must be willing to find ways to share. Read that verse again.

Is our priority to please God?

Have you considered the fact that your sharing means something to the Creator of the Heavens and Earth? He even **orders** us "to do good and to share." I want to please Him how He desires. How about you? Look for ways to share with your spouse, children, friends, co-workers. How about doing "good" to strangers? Those who might be hoping for someone to respond to those deep cries inside that no one hears. Our spirit needs to be attentive to the Lord when He says, "Look, hear, respond."

In Luke 18:35-19:28 as Jesus walked through the hustle and bustle of the busy streets of Jericho, He saw Zacchaeus, a hated, rich, tax collector, perched in a tree. Jesus said, "Come down. Let's eat." Jesus was saying, "Let me speak into your situation and change you." God loves to work through His people and create opportunities for us to do good, share and love His people. Remember, Jesus would leave the 99 for the 1. We need that mentality to go after the one. Let's look for one person each day so we don't neglect to please God.

Go get a smoothie, find someone and share it. :)

Loving and pleasing God by sharing,

NOTES

_____

_____

_____

_____

_____

_____

_____

_____

_____

_____

_____

_____

_____

_____

_____

_____

_____

_____

_____

Where are you serving the Lord today? Are you in a land far away from America, serving Him in a place I wouldn't even know geographically? Then again, maybe you are serving in your hometown. Either way, you are there on purpose. God has positioned you there to fulfill His purpose. Are you in a place that once was thrilling and new, but now seems so ordinary? Are you feeling anything but excited?

Remember the first time you arrived wherever here is. The nervous excitement? The dreams about what this adventure would be? Now that time has passed, has your adventure become like a boring cup of coffee that you couldn't care less if you ever drank again? So if you think your passion is lacking, what are you going to do about it? Don't let time dull or eliminate the excitement, the passion you once had.

You actually are placed to make a difference. You are called. You are equipped to be a light. To be salt. To change the course of history of a person, town, community, church, etc. Repeat after me, "I am called, I am here to change lives. I am here to pray for the sick. I am here to lead people to Jesus. I am here to serve."

If you need to refresh your calling, here are a few ways to try: One, talk about what you are doing. Call someone and rehearse your purpose. Tell them what excites you. Ask your friend to pray for the passion to burn afresh within you.

Serving God should never be boring.

It might seem difficult, overwhelming, and you might need bravery and complete trust in the Lord, but never boring. Never boring. Too many people live day after day never living in the fullness of the adventure that God has for them. I am praying for you to have a renewed passion to serve God wherever you are.

Two, pray for those you serve with. Ask God to stir passion in their hearts. One little flame can cause a whole forest fire. Praying for their passion will ignite yours too.

Three, ask God to refresh you with answers to prayers. Step up your faith by stepping out. Pray for someone's healing, salvation, or deliverance. Put into action Jesus' mission: For the Son of Man came to seek and save the lost. (Luke 19:10)

Four, love the people that surround you, love the unlovely, love the impatient, love the weak, love beyond measure. Don't be held back by anything that causes you to lose your passion. You have only one life. Live it boldly by God's strength.

I get it. You are tired. You have been faithful. You have pushed...and you feel it has been without success. God knows you and had Paul write this just for you:

And let us not grow weary of doing good, for in due season we will reap, if we do not give up. So then, as we have opportunity, let us do good to everyone, and especially to those who are of the household of faith. Galatians 6:9-10

Don't let stress and pressure cause you to quit. We need each other to keep pressing into the 'so much more.' Instead,

Press on toward the goal for the prize of the upward call of God in Christ Jesus.
Philippians 3:14

The lost need your testimony of a life lived without boundaries, a life lived without becoming boring. Someone is longing to hear of a life well-lived, with exuberance and delight in every encounter. Look for that someone, then another and another. You carry something no one can get just anywhere.

Live Life!

Live that love.

Live that uniqueness.

NOTES

_____

_____

_____

_____

_____

_____

_____

_____

_____

_____

_____

_____

_____

"Hi!" from the soccer field. Currently, I'm sitting on the sidelines. **I HATE the sidelines!** It is so difficult wanting to play, but my ankle says otherwise. Anyway, God knows, and I trust Him. I am not here to complain about not playing soccer, but encourage you to cast off any weight or hindrance and get in the game of life. Sideliners tend to watch and not play; they have all kinds of reasons, or excuses like:

I can't.

Not qualified.

Over qualified.

Hurt.

Embarrassed.

Too messed up.

Someone else to play.

On and on....

Excuse after excuse...

When you are not active or playing (meaning being in the game) you leave a hole (big Giant GAP). We're down a player. We are all on the same team, same mission, yet most likely in different arenas. We are all in it for the same reason, too— Jesus. God's team needs us more and more as the time grows shorter and shorter... So, what will you do to strengthen the team?

> *But we will not boast beyond limits, but will boast only with regard to the AREA OF INFLUENCE God assigned to us, to even reach you. 2 Corinthians 10:13*

God has assigned you to an area of influence. You are not where you are by accident. You are called. You are positioned. Friend, your area needs you in order to thrive. Your assignment is to be fully invested... You can't watch it from the sidelines. Your faith needs you to be activated. Faith isn't even faith until it is acted on.

> *We do not boast beyond limit in the labors of others. But our hope is that as your faith increases, our area of influence among you may be greatly enlarged. 2 Corinthians 10:15*

God wants your faith to increase your area of influence. When I play soccer, I don't want anything left inside of me that I can play out on the field, same in my life with Jesus... I don't want anything left inside of me that could change the earth before I go home to Jesus. Therefore I must do all I'm called to do.

David is a biblical personage whose faith increased his area of influence! He did all that God asked of him and completed his assigned purpose in his generation...

> *For David, after he had served the purpose of God in his own generation, fell asleep and was laid with his fathers... Acts 13:36*

*And when he had removed him, he raised up David to be their king, of whom he testified
and said, "I have found in David the son of Jesse a man after my heart,
who will do all my will. Acts 13:22*

David had a purpose in his own generation. Are we serving the purpose in this generation? One of my desires is for God to say that about me, what he said of David. I want God to be able to trust me to do His will and fulfill his plan. This means I have to live fully- ALL IN. I cannot make an excuse day after day. It might be easy to pull back, lay low or even watch others. The sidelines seem so comfortable. But friend, so many do not know Jesus, or are in need of freedom, and we carry the Truth. If not for us, this generation may never rise to its destiny. Let's get in the GAME!

...convicted,

NOTES

_____

_____

_____

_____

_____

_____

_____

_____

_____

_____

_____

_____

Pull out your Bible, read through the book of Jonah. (It's only 4 chapters.) I imagine you have at least heard of the guy who was swallowed by a great fish and lived to tell about it. That guy Jonah. His story can be looked at from several sides, depending on who is telling the story. I want to try to retell their story from God's perspective, instead of Jonah's:

Read this as if God is telling you about Jonah.

Jonah, I love this guy; he is my friend. He is My partner in spreading who I am and My Message to the people of Nineveh. He has attitude, pride, some unique issues, but I can work with all that. I love seeing him walk with Me. I actually have specific plans for him. I want to do life with him. One day while we were talking, I asked something of him that I knew would be hard for him. I knew He wasn't going to be too happy, but I wanted to be for him what he couldn't be for himself and I wanted him to trust Me Completely, learn to depend on Me. But instead, he started running. He ran, like I wasn't faster. He hid, like I couldn't see. He slept, like I didn't know his dreams. I made the winds do something bold, so he couldn't run, hide or sleep anymore. I wanted him to know that I was greater than anything he knew. Instead of coming back to me, he wanted to die; but to die was to be with me, and I wanted more for Jonah. I didn't want someone else, I wanted Jonah. When he chose to fall through the water, hoping to sink and never be seen again, I called one of my hidden giants of the sea to swallow him. I created the space in this fish stomach to protect My friend, Jonah. My friend needed to see My Great Grace.

The moment He cried out to me from the fish's belly, I answered. I loved hearing those first few words off his tongue mingled with water and fear. I love that He knew Me enough to call. In that moment, I was right there. I was in the darkness, holding him together. And just like that, I spoke to that fish… you probably wonder what fish language is… that will be for another time. It just so happens I told that fish to vomit out my Jonah… It wasn't pretty, but it was a magnificent sight. He was the first man to live in the belly of a fish. I told him I still wanted him to go to Nineveh. This time he started walking to Nineveh without hesitating. I love that we now walked together into that great city. He spoke My words that I filled with power. Those words I filled with mercy. Those words I filled with grace. He walked through the city accompanied with My power and Grace, and yet, he was still a little sour. By hearing and obeying, Nineveh became mine. I wanted Jonah to see My heart for the people, their journey, and the great change…too. Instead, he walked outside the city and sat. The day was hot, so I made a plant to grow up quickly to give him necessary shade. Jonah was happy at the sight of this plant. I delighted in his joy, but his joy should have been at the repentance of Nineveh, not at the plant.

I sent a worm, a hungry little bug who ate the plant that shaded Jonah. The next day got hot too. The hotter it got, the hotter Jonah got. He said he wanted to die again. I talked to Jonah again of my love, my love for him and people that far exceeds the love for plants of the earth. At that point, Jonah got the picture;

He felt my heart inside his, I knew that he would remember that feeling and we could continue to walk together. I love Jonah. Jonah didn't choose me; I chose him. To soften his heart, to make him part of My mercy in action. I chose to move earth and the things of earth. I wouldn't relent. I never will relent.

God won't relent in His pursuit of you.

He has called you today. His plan for you isn't going to be filled with any other person. He wants you. Don't think that you can run, and God will just say, "I'll find someone else." Follow His remarkable plan for YOU.

...for I knew that you are a gracious God,and merciful, slow to anger and abounding in steadfast love, and relenting from disaster. Jonah 4:2

You are relentlessly being pursued for His purpose,

NOTES

_____

_____

_____

_____

_____

_____

_____

_____

_____

_____

_____

_____

Messaging one of my friends, I asked her, "How is your heart?" She responded... "I'll answer if you do?"

So I answered: Messy. Feeling frustrated. Wondering. Somewhat overwhelmed with the unknown. Hurting. Sorrowful. Feeling undeserving. Moments of thinking God is mad at me. Wanting more. Hungry. Beating. Longing. Full of love. Questioning...

My friend told me how her heart was... (with her permission):

> I've been feeling weird lately. I don't know how to explain it. Wanting more, craving more, wanting to be used by the Lord more... Am I living with enough compassion? Am I loving people around me enough? Why aren't I talking about Jesus more with my friends who aren't saved? What if they aren't in heaven? Am I truly living for Christ at my true, full potential? Am I wasting life by not doing college yet? What am I doing with my life? I don't know, I guess it's okay. Just needs more encouragement. -My friend.

Her response challenged me to encourage more. I wanted to increase my encouragement level for my circle to be more constant, genuine, and generous.

...but encouraging one another, and all the more as you see the
Day drawing near. Hebrews 10:25b

Friend, "How's your heart?"

Send me a note. Be Honest. Be Real. Be open.

Pause and think about that question. Take time to process it. Let what's hard, weighty, overwhelming or anything else be acknowledged. Be real and honest. God loves when we are honest with Him. This is my push for you today, ask someone how their heart is. Be willing to listen with love. Love them like you want to be loved. Then be willing to share your answer to the same question. Be real and open. After you talk about your answers, pray and encourage them just where he/she is. Their heart is precious, cherished, valued and loved by God.

So above all, guard the affections of your heart, for they affect all that you
are. Pay attention to the welfare of your innermost being,
for from there flows the wellspring of life. Proverbs 4:23

The hearts lead us on the path of life, so be gentle and caring with others and yourself. Trust someone with your heart but not everyone... don't blast it out on social media. Have a real face-to-face conversation, if you possibly can, not through a screen. Lay your hands on your friend, and pray over their heart. Let this connection become a regular occurrence. Plan to do weekly heart checks for friends, family, children, siblings, whoever God lays on your heart.

Friends, let's get past the surface and really encourage someone. We can start by sending a note, a text, make a phone and call, or send a carrier pigeon.

Please friend, your encouragement could immediately make someone feel less alone in their situation. Let God speak through you... He needs a mouth, a handshake, a hug and He's asking us to be that for Him.

Be available. Cultivate purpose in your encouragement. Please do it more!!

I hope you are encouraged... I would love to hear how your heart is. :)

NOTES

_____

_____

_____

_____

_____

_____

_____

_____

_____

_____

_____

_____

_____

_____

dear friend

Are you married? How long have you been married? What's the condition of your marriage? Has it hit lulls of dullness and difficulty? Do you wonder if things will change... longing for it to be exciting once again? Have you heard the sound of the door closing? Felt the hurt of that sound in your heart? Are you so cold to your spouse you could live in a freezer section and never feel the chill? Or are you sitting waiting to be touched, cared for, or loved? Are you crying, giving up? Are you considering texting someone you shouldn't? Have you facebooked-stalked someone that doesn't deserve your attention?

I know how difficult it is if you answered "yes" to any of those questions. You are not alone. Many married people, at one point or another, have experienced the above situations and emotions.

In my marriage to Romaro, we hit hard places (multiple times). Everything seemed to be crumbling beneath us. It seemed like it would have been easy to throw in the towel and let go. But God never stopped working on my heart; He never let go of us. He kept uncovering places that needed attention in our relationship. As I became more and more real (meaning honest) with the Father, He brought healing to the hurting places in our marriage. God kept relentlessly pursuing me, which caused Romaro and I to draw closer. I had to face and forgive myself for things in my past and walk out forgiveness toward Romaro for things in his past. As I chose to close doors to past mistakes, as new doors of adventure, trust and friendship opened in our marriage.

What absolutely revolutionized my relationship with Romaro was our decision to begin praying together. Seems simple right?? Nope! Praying together was actually the hardest thing to do. If I would have allowed my feelings to get involved, I would never have seen God move (don't let your feelings become an enemy to God's plan).

First things first. **The enemy is Real, and coming after your marriage.** He is going to do anything to prevent you from praying together.

So, here is how that all went down: We decided we would start praying together. You did see that "WE" decided to pray, RIGHT??? What happened BEFORE "we" agreed, was this:

I asked Romaro one night, before bed, if he wanted to pray together... all of a sudden he was super upset: "Bec, Now?! No! I don't want to pray!!"

He didn't want to pray now and not in five minutes. Truthfully, perfect or good timing doesn't exist. You have to press and go after it. His resistance was my first clue that we were called to pray together. I realized the battle or disagreements weren't about me, but rather about what God would do when we prayed. I chose to be persistent and we prayed that night rather quickly (what a smile and kiss will do!). Another time, we were praying and while I was speaking, he was snoring... FOR REAL????!!?! "Am I that boring?" was my first thought. It was frustrating because he had no problem staying awake into the wee hours playing video games. But I wouldn't relent...

Our prayers grew as we continued to pray, then developed into a deeper love for one another. As I listened to Romaro praying his heart out before the Father, we linked arms and connected on a deeper level. God expanded my heart to include Romaro's concerns. As we grew more comfortable praying together, private worship time naturally evolved and became some of my fondest memories. Having prayer and worship as a part of our relationship was key when we faced the hardest challenges of his sickness. Being established together in prayer became a strong defense and help for one another. Even in the hospital rooms, we prayed and worshiped. At one incredibly hard moment, we linked hearts and prayed in the hospital room, the intimacy we had with God and one another was priceless, rich and sweet. I am so thankful that we pushed through those awkward moments of prayer, the rough places, the feelings of discouragement that could have kept us apart. We pushed past our enemies and gained a richness we didn't know that God intended for marriage. If you and your spouse don't pray or talk to God together, please begin.

Is there struggle in your sex life?? Start praying together. I can't tell you how much our sex life inproved as our prayer life did. There is a connection. Change your most intimate of relationships by praying together. Don't let prayer become the last thing you try, make it the first step into a new space of freedom, love, and life in your marriage. Marriage is such a gift. I once had the good, the bad and the ugly of marriage, and it is all a gift! Being a wife is a gift. Being a husband is a gift.

Marriage might not be there tomorrow, so treasure it. Work at it. Live in it. Love through it. Establish praying together because you need it! Ephesians 5:22-33

Praying for your marriage,

Love
Rebecca

NOTES

---

dear friend

Are you currently waiting on the Lord for an answer to one of these questions:

What's my next step?

Should I buy this?

Where do I move? House or apartment?

Should I marry him/her?

Do you want me to go to this school or that one?

God hears so many questions from me. Constantly. Countless questions. I should count how many questions I ask in one day. A poll could be fun... Are you like me— do you ask more and more and listen less and less?

"And now, O sons, listen to me, and be attentive to the words of my mouth." Proverbs 7:24

Currently, I want God to tell me what to do on multiple fronts, just wishing I could hear Him. But then I think, "Have I given Him space to speak to me? Or have I just thrown up questions like confetti, not expecting to get a response and/or willing to wait for the answer?"

> *"Call to me and I will answer you, and will tell you great and hidden things*
> *that you have not known." Jeremiah 33:3*

God is a person, and loves talking to His people. He waits for the right time to respond to us. He created space in the cool of the day to converse with Adam and Eve. He walked on the road with Abraham. He responded to Gideon's questions and excuses. He answered Samson's parents. God didn't think, "Why are they asking another question?! How much do they need? Ugh!" He loves walking with us and talking with us. Do we take steps to have time for open conversations with our Father God?

Recently, I was texting with a friend and told her, "I am going to be honest and I don't want to have a conversation about this." I just wanted to have someone listen without trying to solve the problem at hand. She respected my demand as I completely closed the door to her input. A few hours later she texted me with the same boundaries... and I hated it. I wanted to converse and she didn't want to. I trust her and I value her opinion... yet I closed the door so did she, too. When we frame our conversation to stay in control of what is said, and the path it takes, we also choose what we are willing to hear. When we choose not to trust, we are choosing to lose out because we never find what someone could give us.

I sometimes wonder how many times I use my prayers to vent, then close the door to God's input.

Do I really trust and value God's answer, yet close the door too soon? We should see our prayer/conversations with God as a relationship. A relationship that goes deeper than our pleading and desires, but instead an exchange of information for wisdom, leading to revelation, courage, and more. God does nothing that is not for our good! He is consistently for us! Knowing this, we have to keep the door of our heart open. Ask yourself if you truly trust God and what He could say to you. Do you fully believe that whatever He says or does is for your good? If your answer was "Maybe," what's holding you back from listening? Is it fear of what He might say? Or could it be that the answer didn't come in an instant in our microwave world?

When you text someone, do you text them and delete the feed with no response or do you listen for the "ding" and a response? Have you ever waited by your phone to check for a response because you actually desire a conversation? Then why would we treat our relationship with God any differently from a friend on a phone? When we ask, we don't assume our friend's answer but wait even if we have to be patient, because their input is so important to us.

God wants that same kind of relationship. Constant conversation— willingness to be heard and to listen. Today, talk to God much as you would a friend. Talk out your feelings. Talk out your actions. Talk out your fears. Talk out your questions. Then pause. Listen for His voice.

Listening for that Heavenly ding...

Becca

NOTES

_____

_____

_____

_____

_____

_____

_____

There are times when my faith hits a WALL. It's an internal wall of my past experiences. My past failures. If I allow my past to dominate, the victory that faith has planned for me won't become my present.

The truth is:

Faith can be as tiny as a mustard seed.

Faith causes nothing to be impossible.

Faith moves mountains.

My walls are built with the bricks created from the 'why' and 'what' that says my faith was not enough as I faced my husband's sickness. When I needed a miracle, my faith didn't move the mountain of sickness, at least how I saw it. I wondered if my faith failed him. One brick added to another and a wall was created. Can you identify with my struggle? Do your walls stop faith from being active in your present?

Is our faith about getting our way or pleasing God?

> *...but my righteous one shall live by faith, and if he shrinks back,*
> *my soul has no pleasure in him. Hebrews 10:38*

Is your desire that your faith should please God, or are you just seeking the outcome? We can't only be "users" of our faith for the answer we want, when God desires our lives to please Him by living by faith. God gives each of his children "a measure of Faith"...a gift that enables us to believe.

If you carry a measure of faith inside, then you have opportunities to use that faith. You can't leave unused faith inside of you. Let me explain. If you have a cup of faith, use the whole cup. Don't leave a drop in the cup, not even for one day. Do you think, "If I use my faith in this situation, then I won't have it when I really, REALLY need it." That is wrong thinking. You don't have to store it, to save it only for huge miracles. God tells us:

> *And he said to them, "Pay attention to what you hear: with the measure you use, it will be*
> *measured to you, and still more will be added to you. For the one who has, more will be*
> *given, and from the one who has not, even what he has will be taken away. Mark 4:24-25*

As you use your faith, it will not be depleted but will continue to be replenished. If you allow your faith to lie in stillness and never be used, it won't be there when you need it!

Faith is authored by God into your story. He didn't write your story without giving you enough faith to see you through. He desires you to step and step and step again, drawing on Him for faith to continue to trust Him in the turns and curves of life.

We need faith in Him for the times that we don't have the answer we were looking for, and in the spaces when nothing in the world is making sense to us or when we feel overwhelmed by the storms around us. That's when we draw on faith to look to Jesus and let Him author something beautiful that only He could do in and through us.

Do you need more faith? PAY ATTENTION TO WHAT YOU HEAR.

Do you listen to people who may speak doubt? Or do you remind yourself of what God has spoken? Do you rehearse what you think the truth is or the actual truth? God tells us to grow our faith by getting into the Bible each and everyday!

So faith comes from hearing, and hearing through the word of Christ. Romans 10:17

Let your faith be exercised into your daily walk. Pour out on the earth every ounce of faith God has given you… EACH and EVERY DAY.

EMPTY your faith each day.

God will give you more. Let your faith saturate every moment. If you aren't thinking by faith now, meditate on scriptures. If you aren't living by faith, act on the Word. If you aren't applying faith in your relationships, deepen your faith by reading your Bible.

Friend, as you grow in faith, pleasing God will become your deepest desire, not how many good works you can do, your kindness, your lack of sin, your abilities, or even your successes. The Bible tells us God authors our faith and perfects it (Hebrews 12:2). In all the places we have poured out our faith and the result wasn't what we think should have been, consider that our way truly wasn't about the outcome God was looking for. Perhaps He wanted you to please Him as you continued to stand in faith, regardless. Possible?

WIll we choose to live by faith for the answer or because we desire to please our Father?

I want my faith to be emptied into the earth.

I don't want my faith to lie in stillness.

Ps- If you need prayer, I challenge you to reach out to at least three people and ask them to pray for you. Actually do it right now! We are called to pray for one another. Asking is you saying I believe God will do something and your faith will be activated. If we are never asked to pray or believe… It will limit our faith. Text someone. Even if it seems like small things you need prayer for, it doesn't matter. Just please do it.

NOTES

_____

_____

dear friend

In the midst of my great loss of Romaro, the hardest thing for me was that I had no answers to some of my questions. When people tried to answer them, their answers were hard to swallow and probably not entirely the truth. I also knew that no matter what the situation, God has the ability to change it. The bottom line was, Romaro died and it was not anything I did or chose, but it was. What should I do with my unanswered questions? I chose to rest on this verse:

The secret things belong to the Lord our God, but the things that are revealed belong to us and to our children forever, that we may do all the words of this law. Deuteronomy 29:29

I had to ask myself, "Do I trust God with the things that I don't have the answers to; those lingering questions and feelings that come and go?" My brain reels from the emotional swings: I trust God, then I want an answer, then I'm ok again and I do trust Him, in the ups and downs.

Not everything is explained by man's wisdom or science. Even if God told you the reasons, it might sound like gibberish because you don't have the wisdom or ability to fully understand God-things. Kinda like if you were to explain the details of how a toaster works. The child in us just wants the toast. The question remains, "Do you trust Him?"

Trust in the Lord with all your heart, and do not lean on your own understanding. Proverbs 3:5

We can trust Him. Fully. WIthout having all the answers. We actually do it all the time, just in normal everyday life. For instance, do you worry whether the sun will come up every day, and fret over if it will set? Probably not. You also get in a car trusting that it will take you from point A to point B, but most likely you don't understand how the engine, battery, transmission all work together to accomplish your trip. We exercise that trust element in our lives more than we know or perceive, but it's there. Can you be willing to completely trust God with all of your questions, answered or unanswered? You can't keep thinking that God is trying to keep something from you— that doesn't fit his character.

Blessed is the man who trusts in the Lord, whose trust is the Lord. He is like a tree planted by water, that sends out its roots by the stream, and does not fear when heat comes, for its leaves remain green, and is not anxious in the year of drought, for it does not cease to bear fruit. Jeremiah 17:7-8

Trusting Him with my questions.

Becca Love

Dear friend

Hope your day is going well. I am enjoying a dark iced mocha... and thinking about what it would be like to talk with you face to face; to have a real conversation. Life is made up of real relationships. What kind of questions would you ask, or I, ask and share? Would we end up laughing as part of the conversation?? Would either of us cry?

I had such an incredibly horrible moment the other day with a friend that I literally couldn't breathe. My heart was hurting so bad I started weeping and walked away. I wanted to rip out my heart and never have to feel again. I know real relationships have times where we open up and are vulnerable even at the risk of pain, but at that moment, I hated that part of reality. I gathered my broken pieces and processed through the pain.

As I brought my broken heart to God, I asked Him to guard and hold it. In the process, I felt like I didn't want to ever love someone or be open enough to be hurt by someone like that again. I stood in that position for a few days and thought about the risk versus reward. Thoughts of hurt and fear and love spun around... was the relationship worth the pain?

The more I thought about it, I realized how much of life has two sides in everything. If you love ice cream, there is a potential to gain weight. If you want money, you have to work hard and give up freedom and family activities. If you want children, then you have dirty diapers and all kinds of other messes. Want this? Get that. There is normally always a flip side to every situation. Real relationships are like that—there is risk for the best days to be coupled with the hardest/worst times. This perspective stared me in the face. Did I want to shut the door to joy and camaraderie if it meant pain would tag along? I didn't think my heart could handle the pain it was experiencing; but then again, that pain meant my heart was alive and living in a real space.

Real relationships are so good. They should challenge us, grow us, make us laugh, and feel alive. Those kinds of relationships should be fruitful, not one dimensional. The rich part of the flip side is that all people struggle, have hard days, and can be moody. Together, you get to dig in deeper, grow stronger, and live out real grace and mercy. By that measure, how many real relationships do you have? Have you kept most of your relationships on the surface and never let them get close enough to challenge you? Does "hurt" control your relationship? Don't be the person who says, "I have been hurt and I won't ever let that happen again." Those people choose to control what happens to them and how close they allow others to get. The possibility of being hurt is now in control, closing the doors to hurt, yes, but to joy also.

My challenge is for you to cross over into real, deeper relationships. Risk can make the depth of what you have even more full. It could possibly make you willing to fight harder for your friendship. You will invest more. You will be more willing. The "risk" creates space for priceless depth. Will the good be as rich if there isn't some risk?

John 15 talks about loving people so much that we would be willing to lay our lives down for our friends:

This is my commandment, that you love one another as I have loved you. Greater love has on one than this, that someone lay down his life for his friends. John 15:12-13

Now, that's a risk! Your life on the line. When we aren't even willing to give small pieces for a relationship, how could we even think of giving our lives? This is the love we are commanded to live out. Not a hidden, fearful, guarded and controlled love, but love with the realness that Jesus loved us with. To love with no boundaries, no contingencies. Just simply love, then we can be called His friends.

You are my friends if you do what I commanded you. John 15:14

From this perspective, we see how much richer our lives can be with others. Pay attention to the fruit you could bear together. What places can you grow only within the boundaries of real relationships?

Go out and make friends! Don't let fear or adverse possibilities stop you. Let God love people through you.

Continuing to live real with my friends and let God protect me,

Beccatore

NOTES

_____

_____

_____

_____

_____

_____

_____

_____

I'm excited for today!! This could be the day that changes everything. Once before in your life, such an important day occurred. You were born unique and with a God-ordained purpose on (insert your birth date)!!! If today is your birthday... HAPPY BIRTHDAY!!!

Because when you were born, everything changed.

You are HERE on earth, right now, on purpose. You are anointed, so step into your anointing. God made you amazing and full of wonderful talents and possibilities. I wish you could see yourself as I see you, as God made you to be. I know that can be difficult, so I'll just have to keep telling you what you Creator sees:

You are gifted.

You are wise.

You are called.

You are an encourager.

You are a friend.

You are more than enough because Christ lives in you.

Your life isn't meant to be compared to anyone else's, because your mission in life isn't like anyone else's. If you are saying to me, "Bec, I have wasted so much time and now there is no way." First, the calendar is not a valid excuse. Education doesn't have an age requirement. Starting a business doesn't have time limits. Writing a book doesn't come with conditions to be met. The age at which you must be married, have children or adopt—none have unbreakable codes or expiration dates with God. Those limits and laws are patterns of the world. God lives outside of our time, so what He can do is not dependent on time. Don't worry. Amazing things are possible with God. Read the story of Sarah in Genesis 18. Sarah had a baby when it was physically impossible because God wasn't limited by her biological clock. Truth is, you have God as the most important treasure and source of your life. Money, relationships, even unwritten statutes are all a distant second to your relationship with God.

No one has ever seen God; if we love one another,
God abides in us and his love is perfected in us. 1 John 4:12

You are a carrier of His very presence (He abides in you). Don't let what God is doing in your story get blurred or even buried by pressures from people, status, or society. You were not designed to please people. Look for God's smile.

For am I now seeking the approval of man, or of God? Or am I trying to please man?
If I were still trying to please man, I would not be a servant of Christ. Galatians 1:10

Be fully you. You are loved.

*I thank you, God, for making me so mysteriously complex! Everything you do is
marvelously breathtaking. It simply amazes me to think about it!
How thoroughly you know me, Lord! Psalm 139:14*

Making this day count.

Big dreams...

*Love
Rebecca*

NOTES

_____

_____

_____

_____

_____

_____

_____

_____

_____

_____

_____

_____

_____

_____

_____

_____

What do you do when nothing feels right? When you are discouraged? I hope you aren't currently in that space, but in case you are, I paused while writing and prayed boldly for you. Feelings can wreck us, tie us up and rob us of our moments that can lead into minutes, hours, and then into days. Friend. You are not alone in your battle. I've been there, too, and have learned a few things to help you see and feel the truth of God's presence.

And God is able to make all grace abound to you, so that having all sufficiency in all things at all times, you may abound in every good work. 2 Corinthians 9:8

First, only by God's grace are you not just going to be okay, but you will overcome. With God, you won't just will yourself to smile and be outwardly happy, but your true happiness is found in Him. His presence, the very air you breathe, is Him. His presence holds the full Joy you long for.

You will show me the path of life; In Your presence is fullness of joy; In Your right hand there are pleasures forevermore. Psalm 16:11

Don't fill this space with an imitation that will fade away in a moment. Don't grab for something that won't change anything. God has to be the one you are willing to pursue, even when you don't feel like it. Stand until He changes everything. Let your heart be open to God... the one Who loves you while seeing everything no one else sees.

You are so intimately aware of me, Lord. You read my heart like an open book and you know all the words I'm about to speak before I even start a sentence! You know every step I will take before my journey even begins. You perceive every movement of my heart and soul, and you understand my every thought before it even enters my mind. Psalm 139:2-4

Next, the words and stories of the Bible will bring you to truth. Find a verse to read over and over until its truth is part of your DNA. Maybe you can loudly play a worship song to drown out the chaos of your thoughts. Ask God to show up right now. Ask Him to fill you. Let a believer into that space to pray for you. If you feel like you are falling into darkness, ask a friend to throw you a rope. Refocus your thoughts on the Word. May God bring you strength and joy as you learn to trust Him.

Now may God, the fountain of hope, fill you to overflowing with uncontainable joy and perfect peace as you trust in him. And may the power of the Holy Spirit continually surround your life with his super-abundance until you radiate with hope! Romans 15:13

Regain your rightful position and know God is on your side. If you need to, make that list of all the reasons why God shouldn't help you. Once you have that list, search the Bible and tell me where the verse that says you aren't worthy. Can you find one to agree with you that you have messed up too much? Can you find where God is just done with you? Can you find where He says He will leave you?

I don't want the enemy to steal your day or even an hour.

The enemy might be roaring lies loudly into your ear, but faith, trust and hope will silence him.

Listen for the grace in God's words and let the Lord lead you out of the darkness into the light. Do you hear the love in His voice when He speaks?

If you were to say none of that worked, then try this. Reach out to someone and choose to be an encourager in their court. Encourage that someone like crazy. Ask that someone how you can help. Getting yourself out of the mess can be as easy as putting yourself into someone else's situation and loving them. Pour yourself out instead of expecting others to pour into you.

God hasn't left you. He loves you so much, friend! So much. He loves being with you. You got this, because He has you. If you need to reach out, do it. If you need a hug, ask someone. If you need prayer, text/call someone.

You are not alone.

NOTES

_____

_____

_____

_____

_____

_____

_____

_____

_____

_____

dear friend

When was the last time you tried something new? A new instrument? A new sport? Played a new game? Tried a new recipe? Went to a new coffee shop? (Wait, I like my coffee shop!!) Read a new genre? Written a play? Went to a new store to shop. Why do we get so stuck in what we always do? Don't let your life be a copy of what always has been. Don't be too afraid to go beyond your normal and try something different. I feel like proclaiming a mandate for you to try something new:

Remember not the former things, nor consider the things of old. Behold, I am doing a new thing; now it springs forth, do you not perceive it? I will make a way in the wilderness and rivers in the desert. Isaiah 43:18-19

Friend, don't be afraid to be spontaneous. Don't believe trying something new will be just horrible. (It might be, if I am truthful, but what if it is not?). You could possibly really bomb at whatever you try. You could possibly hate it and never do it again. But what are the odds that you LOVE the new??

God shows us this newness in miracles. Jesus didn't heal the blind the same way every time. He spoke one time, another time spit and made mud, yet in the rolling episode, He spit and prayed twice to restore sight:

And they came to Bethsaida. And some people brought to him a blind man and begged him to touch him. And he took the blind man by the hand and led him out of the village, and when he had spit on his eyes and laid his hands on him, he asked him, "Do you see anything?" And he looked up and said, "I see people, but they look like trees, walking." Then Jesus laid his hands on his eyes again; and he opened his eyes, his sight was restored, and he saw everything clearly. Mark 8:22-25

I have no answers, **but living in faith with Jesus is never boring.** The faith life has moments that stretch us outside our comfort zones into a life full of mystery. However, not everything in life has to constantly change and be different.

Jesus Christ is the same yesterday and today and forever. Hebrews 13:8

God is faithful and unchangeable, yet He doesn't stick with a formula. This means God's answers can come in more ways than one. Don't let a formula be the only way we function, but by faith follow God's plan. Have faith to try something outside of your normal box. Some adventures are more fun with someone, so you might join with a friend to start small:

-Sit at a different spot in church to meet new people.

-Ride in the back of your car to get a new perspective.

-Choose a new mug and see if your coffee tastes better.

-Sleep on the other side of the bed!

There are so many things in the natural and spiritual aspect of your life you could explore in a new space with God. He has mysteries to reveal to us that we haven't even begun to glimpse. In your spiritual walk, you might step out of your norm by:

-Telling someone your testimony.

-Laying hands on the sick and praying for a miracle.

-Going to a park and reading the Bible.

-Fasting for revelation and then waiting until you hear from the Lord, no matter how long it takes.

Spaces of growth are vital in our natural and spiritual lives. Maybe you sit across from me and say, "Bec, I'm always trying new things. I rarely stay within limits." If that is you, I want to challenge you to find someone and invite them to go with you on a new adventure. Be gentle but persistent, pressuring to produce what they didn't even know existed!! Life is better walking with people. It's way more fun! If you are fearful to do something new, you aren't alone. Don't let anything keep you stuck in the old. What if what we were willing to attempt in the flesh was a precursor to our willingness in the spirit? How willing would you be?

This isn't about being bored and/or not bored. Or consistent or spontaneous. It's about simply desiring growth. Adding to your life consistently, not just filling it. Adding expressions of faith, removing our preconceived ideas, trusting God to show up, allowing room for the impossible. In those places, we really have no idea what God will do.

And this is no empty hope, for God himself is the one who has prepared us for this wonderful destiny. And to confirm this promise, he has given us the Holy Spirit, like an engagement ring, as a guarantee. That's why we're always full of courage. Even while we're at home in the body, we're homesick to be with the Master— for we live by faith, not by what we see with our eyes. Now, if anyone is enfolded into Christ, he has become an entirely new person. All that is related to the old order has vanished. Behold, everything is fresh and new. And God has made all things new, and reconciled us to himself, and given us the ministry of reconciling others to God. 2 Corinthians 5:5-7, 17-18

Gonna try something new again,

NOTES

_____

_____

_____

How's it going today? I'm actually in Africa, thinking about you while listening to a song. I'm pondering how many songs we listen to, even sing along with, and never truly embrace, like "Make Room" by Community Music.

This is where I lay it down

Every burden, every crown

This is my surrender

Here is where I lay it down

Every lie and every doubt

This is my surrender

And I will make room for You'

To do whatever You want to

Shake up the ground of my tradition

Break down the walls of all my religion

Your way is better

Oh, your way is better.

And I will make room for you

To do whatever You want to

Here is where I lay it down

You are all I'm chasing now

This is my surrender

Thinking specifically about this song, I ask myself: in what places do I need to make room for God? Where does He need more room? Does he have room in the deeper parts of my heart, not just in the shallow spaces? Does Christ have freedom in my heart, access to my time, gifts, abilities, resources? Am I willing to be completely surrendered? What would it mean to completely surrender every area of my life?

Most of us would say their days are fuller than full, leaving very little room for God to add anything. Our calendar has highlights of what fills every day. But… do you wish you could do all the things God has spoken over you, or would you prefer not to add one more thing?

Let's think of one area/thing God has spoken to each of us about. Then, list the excuses that have kept us from accomplishing that one thing. Could we make that one thing our priority? When we choose to live for Jesus, it can't be only a Christianized statement, a song with words which carry no weight. My heart has been challenged with that reality. **How far does God have my surrender?** Does it sit inside of the fence of my comfort; is it at the gate of my abilities? Do I let time limit it? God wants to break through all of those things and see us fulfill our destiny.

For we are His workmanship, created in Christ Jesus for good works, which God prepared beforehand that we should walk in them. Ephesians 2:10

Surrender is going to require faith. And the good news is, not only has He called us to a life of faith, He gives us the faith that we need to accomplish what He has for us.

God has dealt to each one a measure of faith. Romans 12:3

He created each of us with purpose, skills, gifts, passion and vision to do many great things for His kingdom. God loves to fulfill his plan for each of us. He dreams of the you He created you to be. There is so much good that God wants to do on the earth through you. Not that it won't take work and effort and probably selflessness, too, but what a reward when we hear, "Well done, good and faithful servant." Matthew 25:23

Bring your dreams and lay them at the feet of Jesus. Seek to do what God wants you to do in the space you make available to Him. Surrender to His way. Trust His love for you. Friend, please create space for God. Let Him own it. Let Him have freedom in it. He has an amazing plan.

He also brought me out into a broad place; He delivered me because He delighted in me. The LORD rewarded me according to my righteousness; According to the cleanness of my hands He has recompensed me. Psalm 18:19-20

Surrendering my life,

Ps. Walking the streets of Africa praying for you.

NOTES

_____

_____

_____

_____

_____

_____

_____

How are you?

I wonder…how many lies have come from those three little words? How many times have you generically given a response "I'm good," "Fine," "I'm all right," when in reality, you are not at all?

The other day, I was checking out at a grocery store and routinely asked the clerk, "How are you?" She responded how bad her day was, how many people felt that same way and how horrible someone had treated her. Then she auto-corrected herself by saying, in the fakest voice, "I'm doing great. Life is good." And she gave me a fake smile. I was shocked by the automated response she pulled out of her pocket. But why should I be shocked? I've done the same thing in answering, "how are you?" It's crazy how robotic we are in our response to that simple question. Not even a thought about not being honest. When you ask someone, "How are you?" do you honestly care or are you just being polite? When we roll through the motions and don't stop to feel the tide, we miss an opportunity to bring Jesus into someone's hard time.

"How are you?" you ask. Perhaps we can change our automated response to one that breathes life. Maybe, I'm not ok, but I'm hopeful. Instead of, "I'm fine," which may not be reality, how about "I'm thankful," "I'm fruitful," "I'm remaining faithful." These responses can be true and don't have to be a lie. (If you are fine, that's wonderful and I'm so happy for you.)

After Romaro died, someone asked me every day, "How are you?" Every day, my response was, "I'm ok." One day, something good happened just as that person texted me, and my response was, "I'm good." Because I was good. The person actually noted that it was the first time I responded "good" since Romaro had passed away.

I just heard from someone (person A) whose friend (person B) passed away by suicide. But the day before, person A asked person B, "How are you?" Person B responded, "I'm fine." Obviously person B was not fine, so why was the automatic answer given? No one can know what went through their mind that wouldn't reach out for help, but do you ever wish from time to time, someone would read behind the lines of your response to the real answer?

What if we invested ourselves? What if we asked from a place of love, concern, compassion, and responded in the same way? Ask because we want to know the truth. Care beyond brief moments. And let our care be consistent.

People need us to care, like Jesus. We need people to care, like Jesus.

God calls us to be compassionate. Looking at the stories of Jesus as He encountered people…He cared beyond the surface into the real. To the woman at the well in John 4:1-26, He could have said, "How are you?" And she could have said, "I'm fine." And life would have gone on. But the impact of Jesus was powerful when He pushed beyond,

"How are you?" to who she was. His concern for her went into what he offered her, which was all of Himself— LIVING WATER. Do we offer ourselves to people, willing to refresh them with the living water within us? Let's pause, friend. See someone, behind the superficial, and be like Jesus as He answered out of compassion and mercy. Ask God to give you the same earnest care Titus had.

But thanks be to God who puts the same earnest care for you into the heart of Titus.
2 Corinthians 8:16

Learning to be real in asking and answering,

P.S. How are you?

NOTES

Today I am at a new, cute, hidden-behind-trees coffee shop in Uganda, sipping on a new drink called "Laid back vanilla mocha," thinking of you. It's my last day here in Uganda.

I worked at an orphanage where the babies I spent time with were so cute. Now, I am sitting with a younger woman, who is serving as a missionary in Uganda, enjoying the breeze and melodic sounds of others speaking a foreign language. I've had opportunities to speak into her life. It's been very rewarding to impact people wherever I am.

I wonder how many young men or women wish someone would be willing to sit and linger with them? Someone who would be willing to pour into their lives, or share their wisdom.

With all you have been through, have you gained wisdom? Likely, you have grown in perspective, and you have earned scars and appreciation through life experience. How many of those moments have you treasured, gained from them, not realizing how you could be encouraging, comforting and teaching others? Scripture, especially Proverbs, show the value of wisdom:

Make your ear attentive to wisdom; Incline your heart to understanding. For if you cry out for insight, And raise your voice for understanding; If you seek her as silver And search for her as for hidden treasures; Then you will understand the fear of the LORD, And discover the knowledge of God. For the LORD gives wisdom. Proverbs 2:2-6

Are you willing to share your testimony and wisdom to others?

Remember how you responded when someone shared their testimony of how they learned to walk with the Lord through the tough and the tender episodes of life. We listened, and as we listened, we gathered the wisdom that was sown. In talking with that young woman, I realized how she valued how I learned to walk with the Lord, and was comforted by hearing she isn't walking a hard road alone. Someone else has gone before. God asks us to make disciples. Life disciples.

Go therefore and make disciples of all nations, baptizing them in the name of the Father and of the Son and of the Holy Spirit, teaching them to observe all that I have commanded you. And behold, I am with you always, to the end of the age. Matthew 28:19-20

Who are you discipling? Are you teaching and loving them? Discipling isn't an 9-5 job. It's not something we must do, but we are called to. Jesus walked with His disciples and poured into them more and more. At times, He called out one person to teach. It's the same in our lives; there will be ones we pour into more and more. There will also be those random one-on-one conversations that might leave an eternal impact. Discipling can happen in many ways, but it's less overwhelming when we allow God to orchestrate using us in our own story. God makes it so we can naturally do it, too.

Live purposefully; take advantage of opportunities, large or small. Whichever way this day leads you, share your wisdom, perspective, or the love of God into someone else's life. Don't think that your story, wisdom, scars or faith can't speak to someone, let God be the one who authors His wisdom through you.

Who are you discipling?

Love
Rebecca

NOTES

_____

_____

_____

_____

_____

_____

_____

_____

_____

_____

_____

_____

_____

_____

_____

Hello. It just so happens to be Wednesday.

A while ago, one of my friends told me, "Good things happen on Wednesdays. So expect something good to happen." It's crazy how many Wednesdays I think, "Good things happen on Wednesdays." I even go out of my way to make something good happen for my friend on Wednesdays. That one little statement actually changed how I live Wednesdays.

Could just one creative change make life different, unique, more exciting? Perhaps it's up to me to bring change into my life and not wait for a change in time or place to just happen. Don't wait for change to "happen by chance."

If the people around you change, will you become a friendlier person?

If the amount of money increases in your life, will you be all kinds of generous?

If your husband/wife changes, the house changes, the church changes, will the problems of who you are get better?

We probably wouldn't agree with anyone to that extent, yet we can subconsciously choose to live in that momentum. We hesitate to change until exterior things become different.

> *For this very reason, make every effort to supplement your faith with virtue, and virtue with knowledge, and knowledge with self-control, and self-control with steadfastness, and steadfastness with godliness, and godliness with brotherly affection, and brotherly affection with love. For if these qualities are yours and are increasing, they keep you from being ineffective or unfruitful in the knowledge of our Lord Jesus Christ. 2 Peter 1:5-8*

Notice we are to "Make every effort" to let the Word of God change us to become more Christlike and build the character of Christ in our lives. Part of this growth is being brave enough to live completely present in our life, fully giving all that you have to offer and/ or be the one to activate the change.

Acts 9:1-19 is the narrative of the conversion of Saul/Paul from hater and murderer of all things and people connected with Jesus Christ, to repentant ardent follower of Him. Paul changed in moments when he was brought into the Presence of God. If we live in the Presence of God, the change we need will come naturally. Paul was the forerunner of the faith for the Gentiles. We are the forerunners in and to our generation.

Saul could have given up in his imperfection, instead, Paul looked at his weakened state and knew Jesus was there to strengthen him. We aren't perfect and our surroundings aren't perfect, but Jesus is the perfecter of our faith.

But he said to me, "My grace is sufficient for you, for my power is made perfect in weakness." Therefore I will boast all the more gladly of my weaknesses, so that the power of Christ may rest upon me. 2 Corinthians 12:9

Each and every day should be labeled, "Today is the day Good things happen." Choose to read your Bible and expect change. Pray and expect God to speak to you. Open up your life to be changed by the Master, who only does things with purpose and for our good.

The Lord will fulfill his purpose for me; your steadfast love, O Lord, endures forever. Do not forsake the work of your hands. Psalm 138:8

Friend if you expect change to just happen, you will be waiting for a long time.

Sometimes the smallest changes we make can create the greatest momentum in our life.

Ask God to show you what change you can make. Say, "What is your purpose in this?" "Where are you, God?" Then be willing to hear and move to the space where God is and go forward. He will show you what He has created in you. Let me tell you, it is sooooo good. If anything, Paul's story should encourage you that God can do amazing things in a life, no matter what the past was or present is. Ananias questioned God's choice of Paul because of his past behavior, but God knew why He created Paul and no man's opinion was going to stop it.

But the Lord said to him, "Go, for he is a chosen instrument of mine to carry my name before the Gentiles and kings and the children of Israel. Acts 9:15

If God is telling you to do it then grow, change, adapt. Don't let people stop you. Let go of your impossibilities and believe that God is for you. Decide to grow in just one space. Become the best in your current position and see what God can do.

Something good is going to happen today!

Becca Love

NOTES

_____

_____

_____

_____

Have you ever felt like God doesn't love you?

Before I say, "Of course He loves you. He loves everyone!" and you dismiss me and anything I have to say, answer one question: "How do you know when someone loves you?" Think before you answer—-you may have to define LOVE first.

Will these do for starters? I know someone loves me when that ONE:

1. Wants to stay in contact with me—phone call, text, messenger

2. Does nice things for me

3. Gives me gifts

4. Compliments me

5. Is reliable and trustworthy

So stay with me as we look at God and you...

- God wrote a really long letter to you called the Bible where He speaks through all ages, to all people. He wants to speak with you and will speak to you every time you open the book— just like when you answer your phone or open a text.

- In His letter, people retell how he created the earth for humans and then created man to manage the earth. He walked and talked with the first people, and in His letter, tells about the times He came to earth to help us when we got in trouble; mostly because we didn't listen to Him or follow His instructions. He always bails us out. He sent His Son to take our punishment and pay the required fine. He even disciplines us for our good.

- He gave you the gift of life, of breath, of health, of companionship, of the beauty of creation (and season if you live where I do). He has the gift of eternal life waiting for you when you accept it. The gifts of happiness and joy and peace and love...you get the idea? Everything you have and experience is His gift to you. Each gift helps you grow in wisdom and grace when He's involved.

- He calls you His Beloved, His child, His friend, His bride. He says you were made a little lower than the angels.

- His letter to you is His record of promising wonderful things and then doing them. (In Genesis, He promised us a redeemer savior and the second part of His book is the story of that man named Jesus). So many promises--over 3,000 promises— that He has fulfilled, is fulfilling and will fulfill.

One of the greatest "proof" of God's love is that He loved us before we even knew Him. Romans 5:7-8 is an amazing Bible verse about God's love:

For one will scarcely die for a righteous person— through perhaps for a good person one would dare even to die— but God shows his love for us in that while we were still sinners Christ died for us.

In His letter to you, God said His love is for you, for all and for forever:

*I have loved you with an everlasting love; therefore
I have continued my faithfulness to you. Jeremiah 31:3*

Because He loves you, He endured the shame of dying on the cross for you, when you really deserved it. He took the penalty for your wrongdoings, and mine. Isaiah 53:6

I am asking God, right now, to lavish His love on you, so that you will hear Him calling you by name. God will meet you with His love, just ask Him.

Look with wonder at the depth of the Father's marvelous love that he has lavished on us! He has called us and made us his very own beloved children. The reason the world doesn't recognize who we are is that they didn't recognize him. 1 John 3:1

GOD LOVES YOU.

NOTES

_____

_____

_____

_____

_____

_____

_____

_____

The other night, someone sent me a bunch of texts. The "ding" and "ding" and "dings" were alarming. All of a sudden everything inside of me was freaking out! What was happening?? How bad was everything??? I felt like fear was standing in my presence and ready to chain me and my thoughts to itself. My thoughts were a tornado of crazy. Every "what if" lead my next thought down a path of insanity. This led to even more darkness and before I knew it, I felt sick to my stomach. I couldn't sleep. I felt alone.

What do you do in those moments? Do you dwell on those situations? How long do you keep your thoughts on a death train? I hated how I felt, but my hatred for how I felt didn't stop my feelings. My attention was fixed on what wasn't even currently happening but, in my imagination, what could happen was robbing me.

At that moment, I thought, "I need to read the Bible." There are scriptures that speak specifically to these attacks, so I began with them. (John 10:10, Phillipians 4:13, Psalm 18). If you don't know those specific scriptures, then read anything. The Word will bring peace to your soul. Period. Each word is God breathed.

All Scripture is breathed out by God and profitable for teaching, for reproof,
for correction, and for training in righteousness, that the man of God may be complete,
equipped for every good work. 2 Timothy 3:16-17

I began there. I continued to struggle with my mind wandering between the words as I read. My attention wasn't totally fixed. I ended up putting on music and praying which encouraged me, yet the battle was real. I tried to reach out to different people to pray with/for me and after texting three people and the "ding" didn't wake them up (it was 12ish), I wanted to give up. I struck out with four of my friends. So, I decided to go and pray with myself on facebook live (I had prayed that morning on Facebook) so I went back and listened. It was kind of odd, but I was thankful to have someone to pray with, even though it was me. I still wasn't fully resolved in my position against my feelings. I went back to my own personal story in my mind. I started rehearsing when God was there, when I had felt like this before and how God showed up and didn't let me down. I recounted God's faithfulness, when and where He had been faithful. Reminding myself that my God wouldn't be anything but faithful to me again, even if all the "what if's" happened.

In remembering my story... I knew God was with me, even though I felt alone. I just so happened to remember the days when I could tap my husband and say, "I feel crazy," and seek comfort in Rome's words. The enemy was relentless that night; he even tried to remind me of what used to be, telling me what was missing right next to me in my bed. Yet, God was with me that night and He is my comfort. It wasn't just words. As the night continued, I stood and declared I would sleep in peace. I lay down and fell asleep.

It is in vain that you rise up early and go late to rest, eating the bread of anxious toil; for he gives to his beloved sleep. Psalm 127:2

If you have nights like this- I'm sorry, but fight! **Fight for what is yours in the kingdom.** If robbers came into your house, you wouldn't just let them take all your things. Hopefully, you would get your bat, gun, or anything you could grab along with whoever is with you to fight for what is yours. Fight in the places that the enemy tries to rob from your life— peace, joy, etc.!! Hold your ground.

You own your feelings. You own your emotions. Don't give the enemy freedom to come in and stir the crazy inside of you. Fight him with the Word. It's your sword and legal document to declare your freedom. Give God your praise; let your mouth declare the One who is Peace. Pray and believe He answers. You aren't alone. God is with you. Right there at this moment. He fights for you.

The Lord will fight for you; you need only to be still. Exodus 14:14

I'm always willing to pray for you.

Let's remember we fight from Victory and not for victory.

Becca

NOTES

_____

_____

_____

_____

_____

_____

_____

_____

_____

Dear friend

I had been given a tent, so I went tenting... twice. It rained the first time and the tent filled with water. Everything got wet, I mean everything! It was HORRIBLE! I slept the next night in the back of my car while it continued to rain and storm. We had flood warnings. I lived through it and stuff dried. I wasn't sure I ever wanted to go again.

The next time we went tenting, I checked the weather—- no rain was in the forecast. I pinned down the sides of the tent and anchored it well, trying hard to make it secure. But, you guessed it... it rained heavily and the tent flooded. Water dripped on my forehead through the night, everything, including me, got soaked again! The next morning, I dragged the tent to the trash and threw it away. I slept in a hotel that night. So maybe tenting isn't my favorite activity, but then Isaiah 54 speaks of stretching our tent curtains. When tent walls are pulled back, a new space is created. It's not an empty space. It's space for God to do something that you had never conceived.

Enlarge the place of your tent, and let the curtains of your habitations be stretched out; do not hold back; lengthen your cords and strengthen your stakes. For you will spread abroad to the right and to the left, and your offspring will possess the nations and will people the desolate cities. Isaiah 54:2-3

Is there a space in your life that is seemingly empty? Perhaps it's a space that once was filled, but now is dry. Perhaps it's a new, empty space that you have no idea what to do with. Could it be that God is there, in that gap, and wants to fill it with Himself, a new idea, with a project of His making? What's your space? (Write it here:) _____

Friend, I feel like God can't fill a space that isn't empty. Maybe it is a space where creativity needs to be entertained to thrive. The space is different for each of us... only you can know what God is about in your life.

Pause, evaluate those spaces, and see what God would like to do within them, with you. Possibly, you need to enlarge the space, opening up a place for the unknown, call it God space. Could the space you need to enlarge be in ministry, family, business, beliefs, understanding... I know I'm supposed to expand how I think about writing. As I'm writing this letter, God leaned into my space and asked me to write fiction. I haven't even thought about how that would work. Yet, it is more territory for the kingdom. So I intend to walk with God where I am and where He wants to lead me. I invite you along on the adventure of increasing space for a new God Space.

I'm gonna buy a bigger, better tent... and not worry about rain.

PS: You measure something if it is full, not based on the capacity, but the overflow.

NOTES

Ever take a pic and think you look ugly? A second later, you delete it. Snap. Second pic... your thoughts go to, "I look weird." TRASH CAN. SNAP. Third pic... wrong angle. No picture was good enough and you move on.

How many times has that happened?

What is picture perfect anyway?

In real life you are messy, unkempt, sweaty (possibly), maybe no makeup, sometimes one zit and other times more than one. Whatever it is, life is that way whether there is a picture to live on or not. Life is not picture perfect. Then why are we framing our value in such a little frame which tends to always be filtered? You are not perfect so why do you think every picture needs to be? May I remind you that you are loved when you are messy, imperfect, unkempt, even when you are straight up not nice. God loves you.

Think about how God see you? Here's His measure of your value:

> God has given me grace to speak a warning about pride. I would ask each of you to be emptied of self-promotion and not create a false image of your importance. Instead, honestly <u>assess your worth</u> by using your God-given faith as the standard of measurement, and then you will see your true value with an appropriate self-esteem. In the human body there are many parts and organs, each with a unique function. And so it is in the body of Christ. For though we are many, we've all been mingled into one body in Christ. This means that we are all vitally joined to one another, with each contributing to the others. God's marvelous grace imparts to each one of us varying gifts. So if God has given you the grace-gift of prophecy, activate your gift by using the proportion of faith you have to prophesy. If your grace-gift is serving, then thrive in serving others well. If you have the grace-gift of teaching, then be actively teaching and training others. If you have the grace-gift of encouragement, then use it often to encourage others. If you have the grace-gift of giving to meet the needs of others, then may you prosper in your generosity without any fanfare. If you have the gift of leadership, be passionate about your leadership. And if you have the gift of showing compassion, then flourish in your cheerful display of compassion. Romans 12:3-8

Clearly, I haven't been looking through the same lens that Christ has. The least thing I look at in the mirror and measure is my faith. Yet, His measuring is based on my faith. I look at my teeth, my size, my hair... but not how much my faith is alive and well. I criticize my body, and could tell you each and everything I don't like and wish I could change. Even this morning I was bashing my body and I had to stop myself and change my conversation with myself about what Christ values. Christ asked us to assess our worth based on the faith He has given us, not zits or fat rolls.

That small frame of our perfection expectation changes continually outwardly, but our faith continues to grow and thrive and shine through. Our faith should never be subject to how much we have physically aged.

Soooo, now that we've adjusted our lens, when was the last time you looked through your camera roll to see the places your faith is increasing? How real were you that day in loving Jesus and following Him?

After you assess, decide how you look through God's eyes of Love towards you. Friend, please don't compare yourself to anyone else...It hurts and it's an unreal place of measure.

God Himself speaks of your individuality and uniqueness within the function of life, along with the grace that is needed. Maybe our standard for beauty needs to shift to what this passage is truly saying. Go ahead and reread it.

Fixing my frame; giving myself the grace needed,

Love
Rebecca

NOTES

_____

_____

_____

_____

_____

_____

_____

_____

_____

_____

_____

_____

dear friend

I'm trying.

Trying to figure it out.

Trying to be good enough.

Trying to be like everyone else around me.

Trying to be okay.

Trying to survive.

I mean, friend, if you only knew how much I was trying…(ever feel that way?).

God's heart for us isn't about our ability or our will to keep trying. It's not about how much we can carry or how much we can do. Truthfully- God gives us everything we need to do what we need to do. Everything. You can't love your friend without God giving you the love to love them with. You can't get/make money on our own, because that's Him, too. He gives you the skill and ability to make wealth.

You shall remember the Lord your God, for it is he who gives you power to get wealth, that he may confirm his covenant that he swore to your fathers, as it is this day.
Deuteronomy 8:18

You can't be good enough to even have a relationship with Him or go to heaven… That's all in Him and His righteousness. You can't manufacture peace; HE is peace and, without Him, you wouldn't know peace (1 Thess. 1:1). You live and have your being because God moves and breathes in you (Acts 17:28). He gives us all we need for life and godliness (2 Peter 1:3).

We breathe because He created the trees and plants to use carbon dioxide we expel with each breath and convert it to the oxygen and the elements we need to breathe. He created the sun to work with chlorophyll and many other atoms and elements for you and me. He equipped the Earth and has sustained it for you.

We push and work, yet, is God calling us to stop our striving and just lean on Him? Let Him guide us. Let Him provide. Look to Him to be who He says He is. These are the moments to pause and remember that trying isn't' enough and will never be enough. It's a balance, though. We lean in and press on. Find your rhythm with God. Find the place you are okay trusting when He says, "Trust Me" and you are okay when He thrusts you forward because He is already there. He sends His light and truth before you.

Send out your light and your truth; let them lead me; let them bring me to your holy hill and to your dwelling! Psalm 43:3

Stop trying to manage your life and the universe on your own. "Trying" without God's direction leads only to a place of frustration, most likely to a place of giving up. God is about bringing transformation (2 Cor. 3:18). He, with your willingness, will transform you into who He is. That's amazing! It's Him in us. He steps into us and gives us what we really need. We can't be anything more or less.

Today, let's give God the things we keep trying to do on our own. Just pause and hand them over to Him. Let Him work, create and bring the change that gives you all you need in each moment.

He has created you without everything so He could be your everything as you walk hand in hand with Him.

Lean in. He has you.

Becca

NOTES

_____

_____

_____

_____

_____

_____

_____

_____

_____

_____

_____

_____

_____

_____

I hope that you are doing well. This morning, getting ready, I was listening to a message and suddenly, the Holy Spirit spoke something personal to me. The words God said hit me and dropped me to my knees. I want to share some of it, but let me begin at the beginning.

Think of your pen. Perhaps, when you got up, you picked up a pen to write in your journal. Maybe you use a pen at your desk at work. Maybe your pen is in your kitchen drawer, waiting for your grocery list, or to be used to play bills. Maybe your pen is in your purse waiting for you to write a signature on a check. Maybe it's beside a handful of letters waiting for you to answer. Pens are tools used by someone to accomplish something. Pens carry the power to sign checks, buy houses, sell cars, write wills, make contracts, etc. It's hard to imagine all the different things pens can do without really being able to do anything. The pen is the means to accomplish the will of the person whose hand it is in.

As I was listening to the message from Luke 5, the speakers said Jesus asked Simon Peter for the use of his boat. Simon could have refused Jesus' request. Simon owned the boat. Simon's job was connected to that boat. This boat was very important to accomplish his job. But Simon told Jesus, "Yes," and pushed the boat back to let the lake carry his voice to the people on the shore.

Getting into one of the boats, which was Simon's, he asked him to put out a little from the land. And he sat down and taught the people from the boat. Luke 5:3

As the speaker was relating this well-known story, my heart came alive— my boat is my pen. Was I willing to let God use my pen, in my hand, for His purpose? My pen is connected to my work, but also connected to the harvest of souls. I have been struggling to write. It's been easy to put off. I've been discouraged. Then God spoke, and I came face to face with, "Am I willing to let God use my pen?" I am, but I haven't been. The pen in my hand carries the potential for God to use the voice He put in me and let it have a greater impact. BUT my pen could just sit there. It contains the possibility-- without the power. The power is in letting God have your boat, pen or whatever you have and letting Him use it for His purpose. You don't have to figure it all out and know everything... just say, "Yes."

The story in Luke continues...

And when he had finished speaking, he said to Simon, "Put out into the deep and let down your nets for a catch." And Simon answered, "Master, we toiled all night and took nothing! But at your word I will let down the nets. Luke 5:4-5

After Jesus was done using Simon's boat, Jesus made a casual remark, "Ok, you can go fishing, now." Simon politely informed Jesus that they fished all night and caught nothing. But, tired Simon cast his net anyway... and caught a net-breaking load of fish.

God knows how to take your simple (whatever it is) and multiply it. He makes possible what is impossible for you to do on your own. He takes your insufficient ability and gives you more than what you could dream of asking for.

So here we are:

There are things in our lives which might not be our giftings. Might not be the thing you are called to or the thing you are super good at. Might actually be something you struggle with. Might be the thing you want to give up on. Might be something within reason. You could have a list of reasons why you can't do it. But if God says, "May I use this of yours?" What will you say?? "Yes, at Your word, I will."

"Yes" is active.

The boat could have just stayed there; it needed to be pushed out. My pen can sit easily on my desk and never once do I pick it up and put it to paper. But if God is asking, "What are you going to do with this today? Simon's boat wasn't tidy nor perfect... it was available. Is the thing in your hands available for the Lord? What is that thing?

Today, my pen is in my hand. I have more days ahead to actively say, "Yes!"

Praying my and your YES is always available for His hand to use.

Becca

NOTES

_____

_____

_____

_____

_____

_____

_____

_____

_____

_____

Any parents out there? You will probably identify with me yesterday. My kids were a little bit miserable. (Okay, okay a whole lot of miserable!).

First I tried to reason (not always the best of choices, but sometimes it works...)

I reminded them about the last few days that were very busy, their lack of sleep, and, in all honesty, not the best eating choices. All of which caused them to have a need for peace, rest, and nourishment. It was a fact that they couldn't live well on that day without God's help. I told them all we need to put on "strength," "love," "kindness" — all the things God offers us. I knew we would need it (and I knew I didn't want to put out fires all day long). I decided everyone had to read their Bible for 8 minutes. Not even a minute later, everything changed — a neighbor came over to fix my mower and our focus changed. No one read their Bible. As the day went on, I was putting out fire after fire.

Later, we headed out on the lake to kayak and paddleboard. In the car, they wanted snacks and were pretty moody. I remembered that I hadn't enforced the Bible reading (mowers are BIG DISTRACTIONS). I knew we all needed it, myself included, and it had been pushed to the bottom of the list. We needed the Word to fill us and keep us as we went on in our day. As we were driving, they wanted the Sour Patch Kids I had for them. A light bulb went off in my brain (prompted by the Spirit).

I told them they could only have one Sour Patch Kid only if they quoted a scripture. Oh, there were complaints— "I don't know any." (insert eye roll) But guess what? We kept quoting them. They wanted more candy...6 more verses came forth! (I did hear "JESUS WEPT," everyone's favorite, lol.) I also quoted some and Jubiliegh, my youngest, jumped in, too.

I saw the power of the spoken Word. The power to change attitudes, shift focus, and redirect attention. It doesn't matter which verse; they all contain life-transforming power. As we shared scriptures, we were getting filled with what we needed for that moment and beyond. The car was now alive with the Spirit of God. What a joy to hear the word of God coming from my children (even at the expense of a surgery treat)!

One of my favorite things happens sometimes while I'm on the porch having time with the Lord and my kids join me and I will end up reading some of the Bible to them. No rhyme or reason... whatever I am reading. I love the way they sit and take it in. The Word pours into their tanks what will sustain them. They need the Word of God to be alive in their minds and hearts. Church alone isn't enough.

I challenge each of us to not only consume the Word for ourselves, but to read the Bible to our children.

Be the one that makes the Bible heard in your home. Be the voice of the Bible in your children's lives. Have you made it as important for them to read the Bible as to do their homework? God says the Word is to be your priority for your children:

● ● ●

You shall therefore lay up these words of mine in your heart and in your soul, and you shall bind them as a sign on your hand, and they shall be as frontlets between your eyes. You shall teach them to your children, talking of them when you are sitting in your house, and when you are walking by the way, and when you lie down, and when you rise. You shall write them on the doorposts of your house and on your gates, that your days and the days of your children may be multiplied in the land that the Lord swore to your fathers to give them, as long as the heavens are above the earth. Deuteronomy 11:18-21

Reminding my heart to value the Word of God for my family,

NOTES

I was asked on a podcast about what helped me after Romaro died.

What resources could I recommend? The questions stopped me in my tracks. I told her I didn't have any. I actually just found myself only in the Word. I read and consumed the Bible more than anything else in that season. The conversation continued and I heard myself say, "Reading the Word sustained me." I had never thought about it like that before. All I knew was that my Bible was there and I wanted more of it. Even though I didn't really see it at the moment, my Bible was the sustaining power in my life. Sustaining power. What does that mean? To sustain means "to keep from giving way, as under trial or affliction. To support, hold or bear up from below." The Word says:

I lay down and slept; I woke again, for the Lord sustained me. Psalm 3:5

Cast your burden on the Lord, and he will sustain you; he will never permit the righteous to be moved. Psalm 55:22

The Lord God has given me the tongue of those who are taught, that I may know how to SUSTAIN with a word him who is weary. Morning by morning he awakens; he awakens my ear to hear as those who are taught. Isaiah 50:4

God promises to sustain you and others through you!

Now go after what God could do through you. How can you come into someone's weary place to give a Word to sustain them? The Lord can speak to and through you face to face, via text, a phone call, snail mail— choose your vehicle. Ask God for someone specific today to encourage in their place of weariness. Will you challenge yourself this week, each day to bring a word to the weary through a scripture, a song, written prayer, encouraging book, a letter, a gift, podcast, prophetic word, etc? We can all be God's voice to the weary.

Even your voice has been created for God's purpose.

Now therefore go, and I will be with your mouth and teach you what you shall speak. Exodus 4:11-12

You can't sustain yourself or someone else from an empty place.

Sit with God more and more... Let there be space for God to speak to and through you. Maybe that space looks like sitting for a few minutes and being quiet. Listening is not always easy in a loud world so pay attention. Reread Isaiah 50:4 (above) "The Lord God has given..." HE gives. Partner with Him.

Praying for you to be sustained and to be a sustainer!

Love

P.S. Here is a link to the podcast:
LABI:68 Podcast
by Leah Rempel

Rebecca

NOTES

dear friend

This week has been hard and I am so happy for this time spent sharing the Word with you. Recently I read the beautiful story in John 8:1-11 when a woman caught in sin receives the grace and mercy of God. And we all need to know the grace and mercy of God.

Put yourself in her shoes—standing there accused, guilty, full of shame, a death sentence on her head (she could be stoned to death). She had no grounds to defend herself. She didn't even have enough strength to raise her eyes from the ground.

But God was beside this woman, a sinner. His heart was towards her. He didn't accuse her, but He dealt with her accusers. Each one of those accusers, no matter how right they thought they were, slunk away knowing they were as sinful as she.

Jesus was the only one innocent enough to condemn her, and Jesus was the only one who remained with her. He stood with her and asked her to look and see where her accusers were. They were gone. Not one person who had condemned her remained. Jesus freed her with these words:

And Jesus said, " Neither do I condemn you; go, and from now on sin no more." John 8:11

Jesus speaking those words changed everything for this woman. What would she remember the next day and the days that were to come? Would she remember what Jesus said, or would she remember only the accusations and horrible words of the others? Did she let go of their accusations and cling to all He was in that moment for her? Did Jesus' voice and words cancel all the others? Do you hold on to the truth that He stands with you, in your situation, with mercy and grace? The truth that Jesus paid the price for you?

If you keep hearing the voices of the accusers… give them to God. Keep contending with the Word. Believe God loves you and is standing with you against your accusers. He isn't standing there condemning you. Believe it. As He told the woman (nameless and labeled by society), so He says to each of us:

Jesus said, "Neither do I condemn you: go, and from now on sin no more." John 8:11

His love for you is great! (Just typing that, my eyes fill with tears because of His Goodness). May your heart hear the Fathers heart for you. Maybe just read that scripture a few times and let God's words condemn the words of the accuser as He extends His love and mercy towards you. Your story isn't over, even if your sin seems great.

Now may the Lord move your hearts into a greater understanding of God's pure love for you and into Christ's steadfast endurance. 2 Thessalonians 3:5

May God fill your heart and mine with His pure love.

Relena Gore

NOTES

_____

_____

_____

_____

_____

_____

_____

_____

_____

_____

_____

_____

_____

_____

_____

_____

_____

_____

_____

_____

_____

dear friend

What's the most risky thing you have done in the last six months?

Risks aren't just skydiving, cliff jumping, zip lining, mountain climbing, or other extreme sports. Risk comes in many forms: moving away from where you have lived your whole life, going to college, running a marathon, driving a car, getting married, having children, starting a business or a new job, and so on. **Risk can be costly.** Have you ever risked your life for something? Your money? Or do you tend to avoid risk? Have you ever considered risk in your relationship with Jesus?

Most likely your life hasn't been in the balance over your relationship with Jesus. Yet, others have risked their lives because of him. What would you do under the hand of someone's threats? I read Acts 6:5–7:60 today, the story of Stephen. Stephen was performing miracles in Jesus' name which angered a sect of religious men who took him before the Supreme council. Stephen answered them with a sermon and history lessons from Moses to Jesus. Stephen stood there, surrounded by hate with no words. Acts 7:54 tells their response to his shining, angelic face:

Now when they heard these things they were enraged, and they ground their teeth at him.

What would it feel like to be Stephen? In the balance of risk and reward, would you be willing to risk your life, as Stephen did? His reward was to see into heaven and be welcomed by Jesus Himself as he asked forgiveness for those who stoned him to death.

But Jesus was the biggest risk taker of all.

Risk/reward is two-sided, except with Jesus. It's said that you know someone by what they are willing to give up; not the promises, but the sacrifices they make. Jesus didn't just promise us all kinds of things; He paid the price for them all. He was the sacrifice. He paid it without you agreeing to anything. He knew what he was willing to give on your behalf. He knew the price. He knew that He would have to bring it all to the table, and He did.

But God shows his love for us in that while we were still sinners, Christ died for us.
Romans 5:8

How do you prepare yourself to risk it all? Luke 14:25-33 lays out what it might cost to live as a disciple. Most likely you will make a one-time decision that will lead to daily, and possibly moment-by-moment decisions. Even Jesus made a decision that, in the garden, He struggled with (Matthew 26:36-46). Without a continual pursuit of knowing God, you won't risk it all. You have to be in the Word to know your reward that exceeds our imagination and is worth the cost.

Knowing risks and rewards will build and strengthen your courage.

Courage to live for Jesus, even when it isn't the cool thing. Courage to tell someone
your testimony. Courage to push beyond where you have been. Courage to go when

He says go. Courage to live out the call of God in your life. Another way to build your courage is building relationships with other disciples of Jesus. We are stronger when we stand unified rather than alone. Find a friend that pushes you outside of yourself to do what Christ has asked of you as you push him/her.

As iron sharpens iron, so one man sharpens another. Proverbs 27:17

You can do it. The risk is worth it.

I'm counting the cost, and living courage out!

Becca

NOTES

_____

_____

_____

_____

_____

_____

_____

_____

_____

_____

_____

_____

_____

_____

Do you have good news? What's the best news you have ever received?

Do you hunger for good news in the midst of all the chaos?

Someone recently told me they keep waiting to hear something good. That struck me. I thought over and over—why are we waiting for good news? Why aren't we the ones creating the good news in our world? Why doesn't good news happen because we are called to do something and in the doing of it, good news happens?

What is good news to you?

Getting a new car? Having a baby? Paying off your college debt? Getting married? Think BIGGER! Doesn't good news need to carry the potential of Jesus encountering people and changing lives? The Gospel is called "the Good News"!! Now how do we share the good news of Jesus?

Let's refresh our minds with God's thoughts as expressed in Romans 10:1-17. (Please read it now). His desire is for all to be saved. The good news is for everyone. So God asks of us who know the Good News:

> *But how can people call on him for help if they've not yet believed? And how can they believe in one they've not yet heard of? And how can they hear the message of life if there is no one there to proclaim it? Romans 10:14*

Reread that verse expressing God's heart towards anyone who hasn't yet heard the Good News. God desires that they would believe, but they can't even hear of Jesus' saving power unless we do the talking. You don't have to convince them, just share with them the Good News. Perhaps they have been longing for an encounter with Jesus, but have not yet heard of Him or introduced to Him.

My pastor in Tulsa always had a gospel tract with him (that he could hand anyone anywhere) to share the good news when he got gas or groceries. He didn't wait for a profound moment, but was prepared anytime, anywhere. If you won something (like a car), the likelihood that you would tell everyone your good news is pretty high, right? So should it be with the Good News of Jesus in our lives.

How have you shared Jesus? Do you have a way that's awesome or different? How have you started the conversation about the Good News?

One day I sat with a friend (let's call her Abby) who told me that she had a friend (let's call her Grace). They had common interests, like business and the creative side of life. But there was uncommon ground that would come up every once in a while--Grace didn't go to church. She wasn't against the church, but more and more Abby noticed their different beliefs. As time passed, they still enjoyed each other's company, but Abby felt the difference more and more. One day Grace asked Abby, "All this time we have known each other, you never asked me if I believed in Jesus or if I wanted to come to church." Abby's jaw dropped, shocked. She didn't know Grace felt that way.

I wonder how many of our friends wonder why we have never asked them or told them about Jesus. We carry the best news, and we don't have to make it complicated. It's simply good news—Jesus loves you and me! Praying this scripture over us:

...that words may be given to me in opening my mouth boldly to proclaim the mystery of the gospel... Ephesians 6:19

Let's stop waiting for good news and be the good news.

NOTES

_____

_____

_____

_____

_____

_____

_____

_____

_____

_____

_____

_____

_____

_____

How long have you been married? What was the best part of your wedding? I was married 4 days shy of 10 years. The best part of my wedding day was being surrounded by so many people who loved us so much! However many years it has been for you, how is your marriage? Wait...if you aren't married, take 10 minutes to pray for your married friends and families. Pray boldly for them; I'm joining that prayer.

To those who are married—honestly, friend, how is your marriage? Are you growing together or growing apart? What's lacking? What's the biggest frustration in your marriage? Do you feel unheard? Untrusted? When was the last good conversation you had with your spouse? I'm asking lots of questions because I want to push you to dig deeper in your marriage space. So really answer them!

There was a day you stood in front of a clergyman, people or a judge, and made a commitment. You said YES, when you were asked all the questions. Where is that "yes" now? Maybe you should watch your wedding video and remind yourself of what you agreed to or read your vows again. Remember the decision. Have you added to the vows you made in that moment or have you crossed out this line or that line of your vows?

Your marriage is on the battle line because the enemy wants to destroy each and every marriage.

He fears the power of your union and does not want you to live it out... not now, not ever. Knowing that, being willing to protect your marriage is of utmost importance. Do you wonder, "How do I do that?" Here are some ideas from my 10 years as a spouse:

Start by living together, and not just coexisting. Touch your spouse's arm (or butt) multiple times today. Then do it again tomorrow. Remind yourself he/she is the person you said, "Yes" to on your wedding day. Ask yourself, "How have I and he/she changed since our wedding?"

Keep asking questions of your spouse and always wait for the answers. What's his/her favorite thing currently? Favorite flavor of ice cream? Favorite song? Maybe ask, "What is your biggest fear?" "What are they hoping to do?" Dig into your spouse like he/she has a treasure inside you want to uncover.

I know your spouse might be the one person you fight the worst with. What was the last fight about? Did it get resolved? Did you hurt him/her or get hurt? Did you apologize? Marriage requires us to grow on common ground. Plants may grow next to each other, but the soil each needs isn't necessarily the same. Therefore, adaptation and sharing is needed for the fullness of growth and fruit. Let God's presence be in the soil of your marriage. God's desire is for you both to be fruitful and multiply:

And you, be fruitful and multiply, increase greatly on the earth and multiply in it.
Genesis 9:7

Probably your soil needs some tilling, and turning, water and fertilizer. Meaning: be less selfish, give more, love freely, open up, lean in, trust without boundaries, meet in the uncomfortable spaces. It's a rich ground when we come together and let God be in the soil of our marriages. It's okay for marriage to get messy. Growing is messy, but grow together and not apart by doing one thing to increase growth: Pray together! Even if it is three minutes; even if your spouse looks at you like, "ARE YOU SERIOUS!" keep pressing in. Don't let that ground remain hard and untouched.

United prayer is a space where you hear your partner's heart and the enemy hates it. You will probably hit some resistance, but decide that you will pray together and see what God will do. Pray before you watch your fav show. Keep it simple and free. If your spouse falls asleep when you pray (that happened to me), don't let that stop you! And don't get offended (maybe you pray such peaceful prayers they relax too much). Press on through. Don't give up. Your marriage is important to God.

Therefore a man shall leave his father and his mother and hold fast to his wife, and they shall become one flesh. Genesis 2:24

He who finds a wife finds a good thing and obtains favor from the Lord. Proverbs 18:22

So they are no longer two but one flesh. What therefore God has joined together, let not man separate. Matthew 19:6

Praying for you and your marriage today. Remembering what it was like...

NOTES

_____

_____

_____

_____

_____

_____

Have you started something and not finished? I implore you, "Don't stop!" Get at it again. Don't hesitate. Don't say, "tomorrow." Go after that dream. Don't let it go. You have space each and every day that could be consumed by worry, anxiety, or fear, but what if that space was used to create, imagine, or even dream? Do you value your ability to dream?

Have you considered that your prayer life walks hand in hand with your dream life?

And whatever you ask in prayer, you will receive, if you have faith.
Matthew 21:22

Pull out the God inside of you into the ideas and things that will make you more like Him. He loves expressing Himself through you! Opening the door to creative space will bring you into a greater understanding of who God is. Think about the possibilities.

Think of someone— a friend, mentor, someone successful in your line of dreaming— to talk with about your idea. It's good to seek out someone's creative side to stimulate your own creativity. I think God calls us into dreaming those things that are more than we can think or imagine.

Now to him who is able to do far more abundantly than all that we ask or think,
according to the power at work within us, to him be glory in the church and in Christ Jesus
throughout all generations, forever and ever. Amen.
Ephesians 3:20-21

Could we have a dream session right now?

1. Let's write down our dreams:

   Your Dream _____

   Becca's Dream— Writing a children's book.

2. Write down something that hinders you:

   Something that hinders you _____

   Something that hinders me— lack of self confidence.

3. If money were not a problem, what would you do?

   _____

4. What would it take to make your dreams a reality?

Making lists like this might seem tedious, but it's also the beginning of a dream becoming a reality.

We serve the first Creator, God, who began our conversations and connection with Him by creative thought and then words. Our dreaming begins in the same place it did for God. As He thought, breathed, then spoke, the world came to be. The Creator lives in you. Releasing creativity to accomplish a dream must be intentional.

Nothing comes without small or great thought.

If you really don't have a dream to release right now, but are open to the process, what if you begin by getting involved in someone else's dream? Helping someone to accomplish their dream gives ground to learn what an incipient dream looks like, watch it play out, and see the fulfillment. This shared experience could be the first step in your beginning to dream and starting to create space for it.

Invite God into the place in your heart and mind that dreaming begins. Ask Him to make it come alive and be a fruitful place it was created to be. I am praying with you for the same thing. The future God created for you and me is full of hope!

God is greater than our wildest dream!

NOTES

Decisions, decisions, decisions... Ever feel like you are always making decisions??? "What do I make for dinner"; "What am I going to do this afternoon?" Life is full of everyday decisions; some that are automatic (It's Wednesday, so dinner is spaghetti...), some that require the whole family to agree on (where should we go hiking?) I started thinking about how I could teach my children to be good decision makers. They make lots of decisions every day, such as: "What do I wear? Pink or Purple?" "Cereal or a bagel, or both for breakfast,?" "Homework now or later?" Each question needs a decision and each one carries a consequence, regardless of how big or small it is.

I admit, I can waste more time than I would like to on a decision that really probably doesn't amount to much. And I am guilty of not making decisions very quickly. I can even get into a fight about not wanting to decide...especially when it comes to where we eat (lol, SMH). So how do I create space for my children to grow in their decision-making skills? What do I need to show or teach them so they can be confident in their decisions?

First, I thought, I'll give them opportunities to make decisions that affect only them, such as, "Here's $10, you decide how to spend it." This lets them see that the decision is theirs and talking about the consequences: $10 worth of Sour Patch Kids will leave you with nothing as soon as you eat the last one, but $10 on a hobby would last a lot longer. Then graduate them to making decisions that affect our whole family, such as, "You decide what we are having for dinner." We could have filet mignon for dinner, but that would take a third of our grocery budget for the week.

Secondly, I can remind them that the freedom to choose is from God; that the gift of choice is just that—a gift they must use wisely for the best result. I can ask them to listen to the Holy Spirit for wisdom and discernment in even the smallest decisions, not just the big ones. I can explain that not making a decision is actually making one and that they can make choices, but not consequences. God can even ask us to choose things that are bigger than us. Check out the choice God gave to King Hezekiah:

And Hezekiah said to Isaiah, "What shall be the sign that the Lord will heal me, and that I shall go up to the house of the Lord on the third day?" And Isaiah said, "This shall be the sign to you from the Lord, that the Lord will do the thing that he has promised: shall the shadow go forward ten steps, or go back ten steps?" And Hezekiah answered, "It is an easy thing for the shadow to lengthen ten steps. Rather let the shadow go back ten steps." And Isaiah the prophet called to the Lord, and he brought the shadow back ten steps, by which it had gone down on the steps of Ahaz. 2 Kings 20:8-11

There are times and places we have to make a decision because not making one is actually making one. That is exactly what Esther faced:

Then Mordecai told them to reply to Esther, "Do not think to yourself that in the king's palace you will escape any more than all the other Jews. For if you keep silent at this time, relief and deliverance will rise for the Jews from another place, but you and your father's house will perish. And who knows whether you have not come to the kingdom for such a time as this? Esther 4:13-14

If Esther didn't make a correct decision, she wouldn't be part of God's plan for deliverance of the Jewish nation. But she, as a young girl, was raised to make good decisions that are God's plan and sought God's will through fasting. In our decision-making, are we listening to God speaking?

In Matthew 14:13-21, Jesus doesn't just make dinner happen, He asks his disciples, "What are you going to do about feeding all these people?" He placed the situation in their hands and they needed to make a decision. God is asking the same of us.

Decision-making stretches our faith and creates a road to walk on.

Faith believes you can listen and hear. Faith to let your "yes" be "yes" or your "no" be "no."

But above all, my brothers, do not swear, either by heaven or by earth or by any other oath, but let your "yes" be yes and your "no" be no, so that you may not fall under condemnation. James 5:12

Will you grow in decision-making with me?

Love
Rebecca

NOTES

_____

_____

_____

_____

_____

_____

Have you ever wondered why you were born? The story of Samson shows God's intentionality for the unborn. Judges 13 is the record of God's plan for Samson's life before he was even a thought in his parents' minds. His mother and father were barren when the angel of the Lord appeared to his momma (not named) saying:

> Behold, you are barren and have not borne children, but you shall conceive and bear a son. Therefore be careful and drink no wine or strong drink, and eat nothing unclean, for behold, you shall conceive and bear a son. No razor shall come upon his head, for the child shall be a Nazirite to God from the womb, and he shall begin to save Israel from the hand of the Philistines. Judges 13:3-5

A Nazirite was a special class of Jewish men dedicated to God; he kept certain rules like never cutting his hair, drinking alcohol, or touching any dead thing. God put conditions on a woman's life for the sake of the child she would give birth to one day. It's incredible to think about God's intentionality in creating a vessel for this baby. Samson was called before the moment he was conceived. When Manoah, Samson's father, received the news from his wife, his only concern was that he wanted more instruction on how to raise this special baby and raise the boy as dedicated to the Lord from the womb because he would be instrumental in saving Israel from the Philistines. To bring justice to the people through Samson, God required something significant. This is not just Samson's story…this is your story. God has a purpose for each child born to us.

> …who saved us and called us to a holy calling, not because of our works but because of his own purpose and grace, which he gave us in Christ Jesus before the ages began, and which now has been manifested through the appearing of our Savior Christ Jesus, who abolished death and brought life and immortality to light through the gospel, which is why I suffer as I do. But I am not ashamed, for I know whom I have believed, and I am convinced that he is able to guard until that day what has been entrusted to me.
> 2 Timothy 1:9-10, 12

What God wants to do in and through you is significant. Have you considered what God planned for your life and what you are to do for the purposes of God to be fulfilled in your life, your children's lives or your grandchildren's lives? Like Samson's parents, we are to be intentional in bringing life to the plans of God. Ask Him to reveal it to you.

Value the lives of the unborn; they could be the answer to bring justice to the people of today.

Be a voice for them as well.

God is calling…!

NOTES

dear friend

Hello! What's your story? Married young? Single mom? Empty nesting? Have a household of grown children? Is your present story traveling, baking, fixing cars? Will you step on Legos today?

Every wish your story looked like someone else's? Do you think, "My story is so boring?" The important moments and the moments that speed by, weave together to make your story. God lives and breathes in your story.

As you look back, remembering, He could be very evident when you thought He was the most invisible. In recounting your story, you might be tempted to focus on the places you didn't see God. But when you see the whole of your story laid out before you, does the pattern fit without Him?

Today, I think it is important to take time to write your story. Whether you are a writer or not, doesn't matter. You need to remember the times God was with you, is with you now, and will be with you, through it all.

Let the following questions be a place to begin. Don't leave out the small details that could make the world of difference as you look for God's presence in your story, write them, too.

What did my life look like before I knew Jesus?

What did I look like?

What made me want Jesus?

How did I get saved?

Do you love Jesus like you did then?

What's one detail that showed you how much Jesus loves you?

What is the best thing Jesus did for you?

What are some struggles and challenges God helped you overcome?

What makes your relationship with God good?

How did you respond when you haven't seen what you expected Jesus to do?

You could think, "I was a sinner, someone told me about Jesus. I asked Him into my heart. I love Him. The end." Okay. But the details are what makes your story uniquely yours. It's the smallest moments we remember when God showed up. My details are: standing beside a hospital bed watching my husband's last breaths as I prayed for a miracle...knowing I had a miracle worker on my side, at my side, and yet the minutes passed, hours ticked away, days turned to months and no miracle. In each moment of all those times, He stood by me. Regardless of my sin, my strength, my love, my hurt, my pain. He stood there with me and held me up. He was there. He promised healing, and He promised to never leave. He answered. HE didn't fail me. By His presence, He fulfilled His promise.

Your story needs to be written.

One word in front of another. Just write it. You might think, "It's no big deal, nothing spectacular." But have you ever read your story to yourself? You might need to hear it. You might need to pull from your memory what God has done in and through you. It might speak loudly as you minister to yourself of God's Goodness towards you. So, pick up your fav pen and write 5 to 10 sentences of your testimony. You got this!

And they have conquered him by the blood of the Lamb and by the word of their testimony, for they loved not their lives even unto death. Revelation 12:11

The real challenge is to share it with someone.

NOTES

_____

_____

_____

_____

_____

_____

_____

_____

_____

_____

_____

Ever get to the end of something and wish you had more? Coffee? Chips? Another chapter of a good book? TV show? Just wishing we could have a little more....

What about yesterday? Did you wake up and hit 'snooze,' for a few more minutes of lovely sleep? At the end of your day, did you wish you had more time? More energy? More fun? More strength? So much of our life centers around a longing and desire for more.

Where do you want or long for more?

When was the last time you wanted more of God? As believers, we need "more" to be woven into our heart as we go after God. Everything we experience with Him should cause us to have a longing for more of Him. Did you read your Bible this morning and just wish you could linger just a little longer?

So many "things" in our lives don't fulfill us, yet we crave more of them. You actually never longed for one more episode of that show...until you experienced the first few. Same with God— as you read the Bible and talk with Him you will want more of Him. The more you hear His Voice, the more attuned you will be to hear Him, not just in the morning but throughout your day. God continues to draw us to Himself.

God doesn't want to be a passing thought, but a constant reality in our life.

Draw near to God, and he will draw near to you. James 4:8

Seek the Lord and his strength; seek his presence continually! Psalm 105:4

What if right now, you wanted more of God in your marriage? Family? Home? Business? Heart? Thoughts? Creativity? What if you wanted more of Him in all the places that you don't think of Him to be? Like cleaning, driving, sports events, grocery shopping, music, etc? Today, each time you feel a longing for more of whatever it is (chocolate, kombucha, sports) why don't you replace it with God. Ask Him to fill those spaces with His presence, love, peace or a Scripture.

The young lions suffer want and hunger; but those who seek the Lord lack no good thing.
Psalm 34:10

Let's go after God like never before! Seek Him in all the spaces you have never considered God to be. John 4:1-44 tells us of a Samaritan woman who was expecting to find water. But it took only a short conversation with Jesus to cause her to want more and she ended up with water that would satisfy her forever.

My heart wants to be so full of Him that I no longer want more of things that don't satisfy.

Wanting more,

Becca

NOTES

_____

_____

_____

_____

_____

_____

_____

_____

_____

_____

_____

_____

_____

_____

_____

_____

_____

_____

Dear friend

And behold, your relative Elizabeth in her old age has also conceived a son, and this is the sixth month with her who was called barren. For nothing will be impossible with God.
Luke 1:36-37

Elizabeth was old in age and probably even she thought it impossible for her to conceive. She was labeled 'barren'. Who do you think labeled her?? Did she or her peers? Her miracle was actually bigger than her thoughts. Her pregnancy stretched into unknown territory.

This miracle wasn't just for her to have a child because she was a righteous person and prayed for a child, but God was orchestrating it for His kingdom. The timing was just right for her baby to come into the world to announce the coming of Jesus. Her son John was called by God before he was in his mothers womb. God had already spoken of John, the voice in the wilderness in Isaiah 40:3. God chose the season of John's birth to answer Elizabeth's prayers. God's timing is not necessarily ours.

When the angel told Mary about Elizabeth, he actually spoke into the doubt and struggle the days ahead would bring for Mary. Because God had done the impossible in Elizabeth, Mary could believe God created the impossible in her. That knowledge of God pushed her into a deeper relationship with God, trusting Him with all the unknowns. He even orchestrated the beauty and connection between them as relatives. God set the stage. God knew exactly who Mary would need in those first few months. In the midst of so many unknowns and so much wonder, the greatest thing happening in her world, she went to stay with Elizabeth. As Elizabeth first encountered Mary,

..she exclaimed with a loud cry, "Blessed are you among women, and blessed is the fruit of your womb! And why is this granted to me that the mother of my Lord should come to me? For behold, when the sound of your greeting came to my ears, the baby in my womb leaped for joy. And blessed is she who believed that there would be a fulfillment of what was spoken to her from the Lord." Luke 1:42-45

Might we live with such a passion to believe! Truly believe, when God speaks things into existence, those places that are beyond our known territory. Truly believe as we walk out those things God speaks to us, whether we can see them or not.

Don't ever label your situation impossible. Let Him birth something through faith! Nothing is impossible, even if you think it is. Elizabeth and Mary testify to this.

Faith lives in impossible ground.

dear friend

Today, I am sitting in Waco at one of my favorite coffee shops.

I am here alone to write for a few days. The thing is, I am not crazy about being alone. Do you hate being alone or do you just wish you could hide yourself in a closet to be alone? Being alone and feeling loneliness are very different. Being alone is sometimes therapeutic and relaxing, by choice. However, loneliness is damaging and stressful, as if you are isolated and no one feels like you do or cares that you feel that way. At times we can feel the most alone when surrounded by people. Those times when no one really sees you; no one really knows what you are hiding. Your smile can be implying that you are ok, but it's just a false exterior. Have you felt that?

I remember standing in a bathroom stall, so alone. Romaro had an intubation after a surgery. And in the hall right outside was a group of people who loved me. Yet the one I wanted to speak to, be with, wasn't available. I couldn't just pop Romaro a text and check in. I'd never felt so alone as I stood there and cried in anguish trying to figure out a way to lean into God; how to collect my spiritual and physical body and go on. I really didn't think I was going to be ok at that moment.

Elijah, in 1 Kings 19:1-18, felt the same. Alone, unable to figure out how to proceed, he hid in a cave; he simply ran from all that was pressing in on him. He even asked God to let him die. At that moment, God sent an angel to strengthen him. God cares way more than we understand. Even Jesus was in a wilderness alone; He was on the cross, alone. He knows and understands the feeling of aloneness. I love that God reminds us:

"I will never leave you nor forsake you." Hebrews 13:5b

A few days after that happened in the hospital, Romaro was actually gone forever. But God proved to me He is always present, always speaking, always loving. I wasn't alone. I only felt like I was.

Take time to listen today. Take time to push the loneliness out and step into the fullness of WHO God is in your life. Take time to find Him everywhere…in the smile of a random stranger, in the song of the birds, in the sweetness of the first sips of your coffee, but most certainly in His Word! I had to remind myself that day in the hospital bathroom stall, **"God is with me."** He was always there; He had people prepared to be there to hold and comfort me as His hands and arms. It may not always look the way we want it to, but God will be with us. He was not the wind, earthquake, fire…but He was in the whisper (1 Kings 19:11-12). God is present. Even on this trip to Waco, God is with me. I might not have my normal crew with me, but He is here.

If you feel alone or lonely, God is with you.

Praying for you with love,

Beccafore

NOTES

dear friend

This morning, my time in the Scripture left me crying. **Crying over my sin.** Crying that I am not closer to my Heavenly Father. Crying for more of Him. This is a good thing because:

When the righteous cry for help, the Lord hears and delivers them out of all their troubles.
Psalm 34:17

God heard the cries of His people in 2 Chronicles 34 where the story of Josiah's sin and reactions were recorded. As the Words of the law were read to him. King Josiah ripped his clothes as a sign of distress, sorrow, and conviction. He knew he was guilty, as were the people he led. When you are faced with your sin and the reality of a living God, how do you respond? Do you run to God, or are you like Adam and Eve, hiding from God?

Let's take a lesson from Josiah who immediately went to God. He needed to know what God would say about this communal sin of neglect of the Word of God (2 Chronicles 34:21). Josiah's heart towards God was that He is to be feared. He knew God would bring judgment as was just read. Yet he didn't let that fear stop him from running to his God, acknowledging his sin, repenting of it, and seeking mercy. God was attentive to Josiah's heart and responded with forgiveness.

Great is his faithfulness; his mercies begin afresh each morning. Lamentations 3:23

God was moved by Josiah's humbled and tender heart and He relented of punishment (2 Chronicles 34:27). God already knows the sins you are crying over, and He wants us to come to him. Bring your mess. Bring it all and tell God how much you can't live without Him. Tell Him how much you need Him. Josiah repented and was obedient to God's laws from that point on (2 Chronicles 34:31-33). Josiah's actions weren't based on a feeling, but a belief. If you have cried and desire more, God hears you. He listens and is attentive to your cries.

Are you due for a heart check about what you do with your sin? Do you:

Cover it?

Make excuses for it?

Run from it?

Let it sit and fester while you try to figure it out?

Face it?

OR, Do you repent and turn with a humble heart?

God knows your sins, and He made a way for you. Pause this morning and read through Psalm 51, "A Prayer for Restoration". It will be good for your heart. The story doesn't end there, it begins.

Keeping my heart checked,

Love
Rebecca

NOTES

_____

_____

_____

_____

_____

_____

_____

_____

_____

_____

_____

_____

dear friend

I wish we could sit next to each other and you could read this to me. Ever have a friend read the card or letter you wrote them out loud in front of you? I have. I wish you could hear the sounds of my heart through the pressing of my fingers.

When you think about the Bible in general, what comes to mind? Fill in the blank before you go on: _____

I imagine your answers will be as diverse and unique as each of you, such as, "a good book," "I like it," "I believe it," "I love it," "I could take it or leave it," "I don't know," "it's the most important thing I own." The Bible is everywhere— hotel nightstands, counters, bookshelves, stores, phones, devices, World Wide Web, backpacks, lockers, purses, church pews, in boxes, buried in the ground, museums. We regard the Bible as always available, but not really valued. Personally, I love the Bible...the stories, the people, the trials, the messes, the faith, the love, the passion, the vindication, the reward, the freedom, the power, the miracles, the mysteries....! I have loved the Bible since about my sophomore year of high school. One of my teachers stirred my heart and my heart has been stirred ever since. I pray God will give you what He gave me.

So faith comes from hearing, and hearing through the word of Christ. Romans 10:17

I don't want the Bible to be a source to reinforce my own beliefs but to stir my faith to believe for more. I don't think the Word of God was ever meant to be just in black and white, bound, and put on a shelf...it was meant to be living in our minds and hearts, in our conversations, in our thoughts and teachings. It was meant to be written on the pages of our hearts and remembered in our minds. It was to be kept alive among the speaking of it and living it in the marketplace and home.

For the word of God is living and active, sharper than any two-edged sword, piercing to the division of soul and of spirit, of joints and of marrow, and discerning the thoughts and intentions of the heart. Hebrews 4:12

I want my soul, spirit, heart and mind to keep the Word of God alive!

I want to be a carrier of the Words that share and exhibit faith. I want to live the Words of faith as if I couldn't do anything without them. I pray His Word would abide in me and you, and through me and you.

Challenge or ask yourself the value you place on the Word of God in your life.

How many days do you skip reading the Word because of something else?

When did you last memorize a scripture?

When you read the scripture, is it with my eyes open for God to reveal Himself more?

Do you believe what you read?

If someone took the Bible from you, and all I had from it was what you know and have memorized, would you be okay with that? Go after more!

Pressing on and wanting more of the Word,

NOTES

_____

_____

_____

_____

_____

_____

_____

_____

_____

_____

_____

A friend asked me today, "What's your best 'romantic' relationship advice?" I paused, "What advice could I give?" Relationships are not type specific; neither are people with their different personalities, desires and baggage. Each person walks into a relationship with personal expectations and hopes. Some walk in blind and others with everything calculated and planned. Some people walk in with arms wide open and others with arms crossed, guarded. So let's begin with thinking of "relationship."

As of today, what's your Facebook relationship status?

Dating?

Engaged?

Married?

Widowed?

It's complicated?

How many times has that changed in the past two years? Relationships have life so they will constantly morph, change and bend. With all those complications in mind, what would be the best relationship advice? I thought back to the only thing I had—the years I was dating or married. What made my relationship with Romaro, my best friend, companion, mentor and father of my children, so golden? Here's what I came up with:

- Enjoy the process! (Wherever you are on the way to whatever you want to become).

- In the midst of enjoying the process, keep God at the center. Right from the beginning. It could be more awkward later, so don't wait. If God is your top priority, He has to be the other person's top priority too.

- Talk about God–what you believe about Him, what He is saying to you–while you are driving or walking, in play or hard times.

- Pray together–over a meal, in the car, about your future, about your dreams, for wisdom, for each other, individually or together. Listen when the other person prays...you will hear their heart.

- Talk about the Bible–what are you reading, what is God saying to you through the Word, your favorite story in the Bible, etc.

- Read the Bible together. (whenever and often)

- Talk to God about your significant other. Ask God what His heart is for that person, how to care for their heart the best way, His plan for him/her.

- Date your significant other- keep it fun, fresh and real.

- Laugh together- LOTS!

- Encourage eachother everyday.

- Be present when you are together, eliminate distractions.

- Forgive. always, before your head hits the pillow.

Once you are in an established relationship and God is involved naturally, He will stay in a common, known and loved space between you and your significant other. God isn't a party crasher or a third wheel.

He wants to be the most important piece of what is happening between the two of you.

IMPORTANT: the devil won't want anything like this to happen and will do anything for you to keep God on the outside of your relationship…so watch out! Know his plan and make your own plan that will keep God in the middle.

Two are better than one, because they have a good reward for their toil. For if they fall, one will lift up his fellow. But woe to him who is alone when he falls and has not another to lift him up! Again, if two lie together, they keep warm, but how can one keep warm alone? And though a man might prevail against one who is alone, two will withstand him—a threefold cord is not quickly broken. Ecclesiastes 4:9-12

Make sure you have three strands in your cord. In Him, relationships are a gift.

Rebeca More

NOTES

_____

_____

_____

_____

_____

_____

_____

_____

I really love that I get to experience all four seasons in Wisconsin. I love unique things about each of them: Winter, Spring, Summer, Fall. Each season begins and ends... continually moving forward, leaving behind what was and moving towards the new. Each is important and each has its own statement. Today marks the first day of spring. Today, in my yard, new little buds on this plant and that. The tulips sprouts are popping through the muddy ground, beside a few little piles of snow. The change of seasons brings death along with new life.

Transitioning from one season to the next comes without our help. It never delays, sometimes overlaps and just like that, winter is over and spring is here. Seasons in life sometimes come and, like the earth, we can't hit "pause" to stay in the old season. The new arrives, unbidden. "Hello, new baby," "Hello, new job," "Hello, gray hair," "Hello, retirement." In each season, we have to find our place. If you believe that the next season will come, then you live the season you are in to the fullest!

While the earth remains, seedtime and harvest, cold and heat, summer and winter, day and night, shall not cease. Genesis 8:22

The next "season" of your life won't feel like a demand if you know it's on its way. God prepares us today for tomorrow; we really don't need grace for the next season until we are in it. Ever have someone say to you, "I just don't know how you do that?" (Like mothering 4 children by myself). It's because they don't have or need the grace necessary for the season someone else is in.

For everything there is a season, and a time for every matter under heaven: a time to be born, and a time to die; a time to plant, and a time to pluck up what is planted; a time to kill, and a time to heal; a time to break down, and a time to build up; a time to weep, and a time to laugh; a time to mourn, and a time to dance; a time to cast away stones, and a time to gather stones together; a time to embrace, and a time to refrain from embracing; a time to seek, and a time to lose; a time to keep, and a time to cast away; a time to tear, and a time to sew; a time to keep silence, and a time to speak; a time to love, and a time to hate; a time for war, and a time for peace. Ecclesiastes 3:1-8

Live in the fullness of what God has desired for the season you are in.

Look for the richness of it. Be fruitful in it, because, in the way of seasons, they come and go.

What delight comes to the one who follows God's ways! He won't walk in step with the wicked, nor share the sinner's way, nor be found sitting in the scorner's seat. His passion is to remain true to the Word of "I AM," meditating day and night on the true revelation of light. He will be standing firm like a flourishing tree planted by God's design, deeply rooted by the brooks of bliss, bearing fruit in every season of life. He is never dry, never fainting, ever blessed, ever prosperous. Psalm 1:1-3

Fully live the peace of your season and be fruitful.

NOTES

_____

_____

_____

_____

_____

_____

_____

_____

_____

_____

_____

_____

_____

_____

_____

_____

_____

What makes you very happy? I love all kinds of things from hiking, skiing, paddle boarding, soccer, shopping, playing games, doing most things outside, and bringing coffee with me to do any of it. :) As we live for Christ, our happy place can be a partnership of hard work and crazy fun. Joy can be infused into all the situations of your life.

> *For the kingdom of God is not a matter of eating and drinking but of righteousness and peace and joy in the Holy Spirit. Romans 14:17*

Do you know that Joy is ⅓ of the Kingdom of God? That should mean something!! As we work and walk around and do kingdom work, we are to be joyful!! How would you rate your joy level from 1-10? _____

> *You make known to me the path of life; in your presence there is fullness of joy; at your right hand are pleasures forevermore. Psalm 16:11*

I don't want to be the "Christian" who, when people encounter Christ through me, all they see is someone overwhelmed, sad and barely making it. Living for Jesus has joy in the midst of life that is real and amazing! Beyond joy, have you thought it should be fun, too? It's not always work, work, work (work can be enjoyable with the right mindset and motive). It's not just a narrow, "no fun allowed" lane. It's not "don't do this" and "don't do that" (rules upon rules).

Living for Christ IS the abundant life He gave us!

> *A thief has only one thing in mind—he wants to steal, slaughter, and destroy. But I have come to give you everything in abundance, more than you expect—life in its fullness until you overflow! John 10:10*

God wants us to experience Him in creation, in games, in all the fun things we do in life. Bonus: He wants to do it with us. Work hard for God, but live with him, too. Each day you wake up, remind yourself:

> *This is the day that the Lord has made; let us rejoice and be glad in it. Psalm 118:24*

Today and each day, we have the opportunity to experience joy and happiness. Can you take a portion of today to do something fun? Then, assess where God was in it. Ask yourself what did God show you in it? I wish I could see all of the fun things you will do today. Be intentional to choose something that you want to do, or something new. Maybe invite someone with you; maybe a group of people to join you for more fun. Before you go, set aside all the stuff (stress, frustration, time, work) you think you should be doing instead.

> *Pour out all your worries and stress upon him and leave them there, for he always tenderly cares for you. 1 Peter 5:7*

Live life! I am going to do that today with you—I'll buy a new pair of shoes! Maybe, post a picture and hashtag it #somethingfun to share with all of us.

#somethingfun

*Love
Rebecca*

NOTES

_____

_____

_____

_____

_____

_____

_____

_____

_____

_____

_____

_____

_____

_____

_____

_____

_____

_____

Loving God and loving people has to be intentional! Sometimes loving God is so easy but loving people...well that can be challenging.

People can be all kinds of different. They can be everything you want or nothing you want. They add the most to life and take the most away. People can take you places you never expected and leave you in places you never imagined. How easy it is to want to give up on people one minute and cheer them on the next. People pass through our life like a storm or settle in like the sun. Friends are people who dig into your heart and plant themselves. And we get to love them. We have to be intentional in showing love to people and be intentional in forgiving. We grow to love people but also make disciples while becoming friends.

The disciple, whom Jesus loved, was reclining at a table at Jesus' side. John 13:23

John wasn't just a person and a disciple, but a friend. People can be like that...somehow they walk into our space and it takes only one conversation for a friendship to be born. Friendship is intentional, it's sweet, but it comes with risk.

I loved Romaro, my best friend, but lost him. We had a vulnerable love, open and real, but at the loss of him, my heart broke. I hurt in a place I thought was safe; my love was safe in his heart. That connection was gone in a moment, but the hurt lasted. Walking on without him, I had to decide, will I love people with deep, rich love, even though there is risk of being broken again? It's not an easy decision, friends. I want to trust God with my heart, but people? I think God let me taste his love for me. God loved me even though I broke His heart by my sin. And then He risked giving His son to restore me... and you.

He who did not spare his own Son but gave him up for us all, how will he not also with him graciously give us all things? Romans 8:32

God doesn't ask me to safeguard love in my heart, but give His love, and let it be real for each person I encounter, loving them freely, willing to risk being broken by them, willing to never hold back, knowing God has a continual love flowing towards me for myself and others. I choose to trust God and His love, then be intentional in loving people. People really are worth the risk, always. I choose to be intentional in giving my love, not letting what happened hold me back. I am intentional, knowing His love can be expressed in many ways: getting together weekly, checking in monthly, texting a prayer, doing fun things and hard things together, being transparent, loving when it's not easy, always giving grace.

The real question is what are you doing with the love God put in you? Don't let people be the answer for your life, let them be the purpose.

Love God. Love people. Mark 12:29-31

Do what He asks. Love when it's hard,

NOTES

_____

_____

_____

_____

_____

_____

_____

_____

_____

_____

_____

_____

_____

_____

_____

_____

_____

_____

CONCLUSION

You friend, get to live it or give it...

Praying for you.

Proverbs 11:25

Love
Becca

Sneak Peek!

.....

Dear friend 2

Coming Soon

Enjoy the Bonus Days!

dear friend

Today is a wonderful day! April 1st. It's full of funny potential. It's full of seeing things a little bit differently. Once, my kids replaced the cream in a doughnut with mayo and gave it to a friend. She ate the whole thing, but didn't act like anything was wrong. She didn't give us the pleasure of the prank. Sometimes something may be not what we expect, and we don't see the reality.

Read the story of Samson in Judges 14 and 15, looking for his playful, joking side. But I also want to touch on another, unexpected piece of his story:

> Samson went down to Timnah, and at Timnah he saw one of the daughters of the Philistines. Then he came up and told his father and mother, "I saw one of the daughters of the Philistines at Timnah. Now get her for me as my wife." But his father and mother said to him, "Is there not a woman among the daughters of your relatives, or among all our people, that you must go to take a wife from the uncircumcised Philistines?" But Samson said to his father, "Get her for me, for she is right in my eyes." His father and mother did not know that it was from the Lord, for he was seeking an opportunity against the Philistines. At that time the Philistines ruled over Israel. Judges 14:1-4

Samson wants a woman from a different tribe, an enemy-of-God tribe. His parents were not okay with his plan. He had been dedicated to the Lord before he was conceived and they had very clear instructions from God on how to raise him. However, Samson's unlikely union was actually part of God's plan. The parents' ability to see was very limited, and they were far from understanding what God was doing. They were saying what should be said in normal circumstances, I'll give them that; yet they were wrong. Samson's parents were fighting against something that God actually wanted to accomplish. Perhaps you are struggling with an issue with your child. Have you asked God, who sees more, to show you what the real issue is or how to handle it? Are you contending for His understanding and mind in the situation? I know I don't want to fight against God even if I 'know' the right way.

Asking for revelation is always a good idea.

Contend to understand and know the whole truth of the situation. There are things we might not be able to understand, yet He can bring us into a place of clarity. Do you have a problem, struggle, or hard place in which you need fresh revelation? I believe God will speak to you about it right now.

> Then you will understand righteousness and justice [in every circumstance] And integrity and every good path. For [skillful and godly] wisdom will enter your heart and knowledge will be pleasant to your soul. Proverbs 2:9-10

God isn't trying to hold back revelation from us, but, without asking, we might never know. He is faithful.

*Call to me and I will answer you, and will tell you great and hidden
things that you have not known. Jeremiah 33:3*

By the way, I HATE pranks. Very, very much. (I wasn't really involved in the mayo, lol).

But I do love doughnuts and revelation.

NOTES

Do you have clothes, shoes, or a jacket you really dislike wearing? That one item that just rubs you wrong? I despise uncomfortable clothes bought because I like the look. I have a new pair of shoes that would fit that description. I would almost prefer to wear dirty jeans than uncomfortable ones. That's a bad enough confession, BUT...

What if the Bible makes you uncomfortable? I was reading this passage:

What shall we say then? Is there injustice on God's part? By no means! For he says to Moses, "I will have mercy on whom I have mercy, and I will have compassion on whom I have compassion." So then it depends not on human will or exertion, but on God, who has mercy. For the Scripture says to Pharaoh, "For this very purpose I have raised you up, that I might show my power in you, and that my name might be proclaimed in all the earth." So then he has mercy on whomever he wills, and he hardens whomever he wills.
Romans 9:14-18

When I read this I got really uncomfortable. It didn't fit my beliefs. Are you thinking, "What do you mean? That's the Bible, Bec! Christians have to believe it." Relax, I completely believe the Bible. Am I comfortable with how I understand some of the Word? Ummmmm, no. Not on purpose, I know there are things that I prefer to believe. The Scripture above fights against the places in my beliefs that aren't yet lined up with the Word of God. It's like sandpaper to my spirit; an uncomfortable pair of shoes. I like the things I believe until I am confronted with lies that I believe. Such as, I like believing that if I am good, God will have mercy on me; and that if I'm not, He won't. I know that is a belief I have been told or I told to myself, perhaps because I like the idea of some control over my relationship with Christ. This verse confronts the lie I have believed and stirs me uncomfortably to fight spiritually, intellectually and emotionally with the comfortable lie. Then I have a choice to believe the truth either about God or myself.

The Word of God will have places that challenge what we believe and why we believe it. If the devil has lied to you and you have believed it, the Word will bring revelation to get you in the line with the truth.

...For he died for us, sacrificing himself to make us holy and pure, cleansing us through the showering of the pure water of the Word of God. Ephesians 5:25b-26

When you feel uncomfortable while reading the Word, don't just ignore and skip over it, but examine it and yourself as to what is making you uncomfortable. Perhaps it's a misunderstanding of what it is saying. Try reading it in another translation. If 'the rub' is still there, let the Spirit minister deeper understanding, breaking off those places with revelation of His Truth.

Let the Word of God contend for your heart space, and meet you in such a way that reveals anything that isn't true, and transform you.

Friend, please don't ever try to change what the Bible says to fit your own beliefs—it won't work.

Kicking the lies off like a pair of tight shoes,

Becca Love

NOTES

_____

_____

_____

_____

_____

_____

_____

_____

_____

_____

_____

_____

_____

_____

_____

_____

_____

_____